Get Your SHIFT Together

Get Your SHIFT Together

How to Think, Laugh, and Enjoy Your Way to Success in Business and in Life

STEVE RIZZO

NEW YORK   CHICAGO   SAN FRANCISCO
LISBON   LONDON   MADRID   MEXICO CITY   MILAN
NEW DELHI   SAN JUAN   SEOUL   SINGAPORE
SYDNEY   TORONTO

The McGraw·Hill Companies

1 2 3 4 5 6 7 8 9 0   DOC/DOC   1 8 7 6 5 4 3 2

ISBN 978-0-07-180773-9
MHID   0-07-180773-X

e-ISBN 978-0-07-180774-6
e-MHID   0-07-180774-8

Library of Congress Cataloging-in-Publication Data

Rizzo, Steve.
  Get your shift together : how to think, laugh, and enjoy your way to success in business and in life / by Steve Rizzo.
    p. cm.
  ISBN-13: 978-0-07-180773-9 (alk. paper)
  ISBN-10: 0-07-180773-X (alk. paper)
  1. Change (Psychology)   2. Attitude (Psychology)   3. Self-realization.
  4. Success. I. Title.
  BF637.C4R59 2013
  650.1—dc23   2012034077

Design by Mauna Eichner and Lee Fukui

McGraw-Hill books are available at special quantity discounts to use as premiums and sales promotions or for use in corporate training programs. To contact a representative, please e-mail us at bulksales@mcgraw-hill.com.

This book is printed on acid-free paper.

To my brother Michael,
who taught me how to
Get My SHIFT Together

Contents

Part 3

May the Shift Be with You

Part 4

The Shift Continues

Foreword

How's your attitude?

Each one of you reading this will have a different perspective on what attitude is, how it is defined, and how that definition relates to you. But everyone reading this book will improve his or hers as a result of it.

I've known Steve Rizzo for almost two decades. I call him Rizzo. I've seen his stand-up act. I've seen his corporate presentations. And I've seen his presentations to his peers, teaching everyone about the power of positive thinking and the importance humor has in their lives.

More than a friend, Rizzo is somebody I learn from and laugh with. Sometimes I even make him laugh. The highest compliment you can get from Rizzo is a laugh punctuated with, "Now, dat's funny!" in a Brooklyn accent.

Get Your SHIFT Together is the essence of Steve Rizzo's thinking, combined with his ability to transfer his message. The reason his message is so transferable is that he substitutes the word *change*, which can be somewhat harsh and normally has negative connotations, with the word *shift*, which is much more positive. Shifting your attitude doesn't seem as arduous a task as changing your attitude.

This is a book that encourages you to think about what you say before you say it. To think about the actions you take before you take them. To focus on what's working in your life instead of fixating on what isn't working. And to find the laughter in the good times *and* the tough times.

Is this a personal book?

YES! It will give you insights and examples that you can apply to friendships and relationships.

Is this a business book?

YES! It will give you insights and examples that you can apply to coworkers and customers.

Is this a life book?

YES! It will give you insights and examples that you can apply to yourself. It will bring you from down to up. It will bring you from "woe is me" to "*wow* is me!"

Over the past several years, laughter has declined in use. The economic downturn, depressed real estate values, the price of gasoline, and the true number of unemployed have caused genuine concern among all of us—and for some, genuine panic.

The beauty and power of Steve Rizzo's book is that it addresses those issues head-on and gives the reader ideas and commonsense strategies that can be implemented immediately, even before you close the book.

But the most important aspect of this book is the fact that it is written for *you*. If you read it properly and implement the Attitude Adjustment Strategies that Rizzo offers, your shift in thinking, which will help you laugh and enjoy your life—regardless of the circumstances—will be permanent.

Why should you read this book and buy a copy for someone you know? As a close friend, I can tell you that Rizzo lives in the positive. I've never seen him in a bad mood. He always interacts with people in a positive way. He leads with a smile. He engages with great fun. His observations and stories about life are hysterical and poignant. And he will always leave you with a kind word.

Known as the Attitude Adjuster, Steve Rizzo has a timeless, unbeatable attitude, and he's written this life-changing gem.

Get Your SHIFT Together is not just a book. It's a gift you can give your family, your friends, your coworkers, your customers—and especially yourself.

Shift your thoughts to positive.

Shift your mindset to happy.

Shift your personal conversations to engaging.

Shift your business conversations to productive.

Shift your family interactions to enjoyment.

Shift your job and career aspirations to advancement.

And shift your life from where you are now to success and fulfillment.

I'm positive you will love this book. All it requires to get started is shifting your credit card from your wallet to the cashier.

JEFFREY GITOMER,
author of the *Little Red Book of Selling*
and the *Little Gold Book of YES! Attitude*

Acknowledgments

My mission in life is to show people how to be happy and successful in business and in life, regardless of their circumstances. This book was written for the sole purpose of bringing hope and encouragement into the lives of those who feel hopeless and discouraged during these challenging times.

My message is a simple one: If you shift your focus and way of thinking, you can turn challenging times into opportunities. If you are grateful for what you have, rather than fixating on what you don't have, you can be happier than you ever imagined. And if you unleash the power of your Humor Being on a daily basis, you will come to know that not even fear can stand against the power of laughter. How's that for delivering the truth?

I was not alone in putting this book together. There was a Higher Power involved that guided me to the right people at the right time. (I love when that happens.) I first would like to thank the publishing professionals at McGraw-Hill, particularly Casey Ebro, Courtney Fischer, Pamela Peterson, Jane Palmieri, and Mary Glenn, for their high energy and belief in my message.

I would like to thank my literary agent, Laura Nolan at Paradigm Agency, who supported me through the entire process of making the right choices.

I also would like to thank my management team from All Parts Move, Glenn Stone and Maurice Keizer. Thank you for staying with me through the tough times. And I mean tough!

I have to thank the one and only (Thank God!) Joe Ward for his uncanny way of making successful things happen.

Very special thanks to my two ingenious collaborators, Greg Mewbourne, for his great sense of humor and wordsmithing skills, and May Wuthrich, whose keen insight, persistence, and invaluable editing skills made this book come to life. You both made this entire process smooth and fun.

To Nancy Lauterbach, who is primarily responsible for my transformation from stand-up comedian to motivational speaker, thank you for helping me realize that I can be both.

To Jeffrey Gitomer, who never ceases to amaze me with his expertise and willingness to help. You are a true friend.

I also have to thank my good friends and business associates Ed Primeau, my video guy, and Jim Barbour, my web guy. You are both the very best at what you do. And you both know how particular I can be.

I am indebted to Jeff Slutsky, whose friendship, advice, and sick sense of humor keep me moving forward.

To funny man Rodney Carrington, we may have a long-distance friendship, but I value it more than you will ever know. Plus, you're almost funnier than I am.

To my dear friend Al Parinello, who was the first one to read this book in its early stages and gave me the confidence to move forward. (And who thinks he's funnier than I am.)

To Joe Fusco, who shares my philosophy in life and taught me how to love my problems.

To Steve Blue, thank you for all of your help and friendship.

To Lt. Col. Rob "Waldo" Waldman, thank you for being my Wingman.

Thank you to all who have attended my programs and have supported me throughout the years.

Thank you to my mom and dad, for giving me life and the wonderful gift of humor. It really came in handy. You will always be in my heart.

Thank you to my brother Ricky and my sister, Laurie, for the wonderful memories of nonstop laughter. Especially when times were tough. I would like to give a special thank you to my Labrador retrievers (my family members), Jessie, Wally, and the endearing spirits of Shelby, Casey, and Brandy. Each of them, in their own way, has taught me how to enjoy the moment, when to take time out and play, and most of all, the true meaning of unconditional love.

Thank you to my son, Sean, my daughter-in-law, Diana, and my beautiful grandson, Julian, for putting my life in perspective.

I don't care for clichés, but I really did save the best for last. I want to thank my wife, Gina. You walk my talk better than I do. You are the ultimate Humor Being and the motivation behind the motivator. (That should put me on her good side for a while.)

Get Your SHIFT Together

Part 1

My Shift from a Comedian to the Attitude Adjuster

When times are tough, we all have opportunities to perform our own miracles. It's a matter of how you perceive and meet the challenge.

STEVE RIZZO (THAT'S ME)

Hi, I'm Steve Rizzo, comedian turned

professional motivator. Nice to meet you. Make yourself comfortable. Are you comfortable yet? Good. Hey, thanks for buying this book, by the way. Or maybe you didn't buy it. Maybe a friend gave it to you. Well, that's good too. There's nothing better than the gift of shift, I say. I take shift from my friends all the time. Of course, it's my job to talk shift, and I hope you're prepared, because I'm about to sling some your way.

Let me take you on a trip down memory lane, where I will reveal why I left a promising career as a stand-up comedian to start a career that I knew absolutely nothing about. Here you will learn how my quest to break through the emotional barriers that were keeping me from what I truly desired has brought my life and my work full circle. It's all about the Power of Shifting!

I will also introduce to you the biggest inspiration in my life. The lessons I learned from him through the years have been invaluable. Witnessing his remarkable ability to shift his mindset in the midst of extreme adversity is without a doubt the catalyst that allowed me to turn my life around and is the inspiration for my success and happiness today.

1

A Change in Direction

In the middle of difficulty lies opportunity.

ALBERT EINSTEIN

In the early 1980s, I was gaining momentum as a national headlining comedian. Many up-and-coming comics like Dennis Miller and Rosie O'Donnell opened for me. On the road, I shared the stage with Eddie Murphy, Rodney Dangerfield, Jerry Seinfeld, Ellen DeGeneres, and Richard Pryor. By 1994 I was flying high with a list of TV comedy specials to my credit. Sounds promising, doesn't it?

Despite this success and after much soul searching, I made a major shift and decided to do something more meaningful with my life. I remember being with my friend and roommate comedian Drew Carey and telling him I was through with the business. "That's it," I said. "I'm not doing this anymore! I'm going back home!" Carey said, "You can't leave now. You're too close!" And that's when it hit me: How can it be that I'm so close to something I don't want? "Making it," to use show business parlance, no longer held the allure for me that it once had. Within a matter of days, I packed my things and went back home to New York—away from a promising career as a stand-up comedian and toward the start of a new vocation, that of a professional motivational speaker and trainer.

Making this kind of sudden left turn may sound crazy to you, but it was reality for me. Although I no longer wanted to be a comic, I still was, and am, a comedian. The funny part of me is still very much alive and always will be. Since I was a kid, whether on- or offstage, I've had the ability to make people laugh. Sometimes that sense of humor got me into trouble, especially when I was young and talking to adults. It didn't matter how serious the conversation was, if there was room for a punch line, I would blurt it out.

One time, when I was 11 years old, my father was reprimanding me for lying. Man, was he upset. He looked me straight in the eyes and said, "What kind of idiot do you think I am?!" I couldn't help myself. Without missing a beat, I said, "Well, Pop, what are my choices?"

My son followed in my footsteps. All through grade school he played the role of Mr. Comedian. This was a particular problem in the classroom, where he constantly cracked jokes. Once when I asked him how his school day went, he was quick to answer, "Good crowd! Good crowd!" Trying to hold back the laughter, I said, "Don't get smart with me." His reply: "Don't worry, Pop, I don't want to confuse you."

Today, I use comedy as an attention grabber to help captivate my audience and get my message across. If you laugh while you learn it's just an added bonus. In fact, if you're having fun while you learn, studies show that you learn better.

Over the last 14 years, a wide array of clients have hired me to speak to audiences across the country. These include government agencies like the CIA, Fortune 100 companies like JP Morgan Chase, AT&T, and MetLife, healthcare organizations such as Bayer Health Care and GE Health Care, regional associations like the

National Restaurant Association and the Association for Office Professionals, and emerging businesses like Heidtman Steel Products.

In addition, I have given my time and services to charities, homeless shelters, schools, and hospitals. And I have mentored those doing time in prison. As I follow my life mission, meeting people from all sectors of society, I find that as much as I may be an instrument of change to the many thousands of people whose paths I cross, I am equally changed by them.

So . . . now that you know something about me, it's time to get started.

Flash back to the mid-1990s and the timeline for how this change in direction for me unfolded. First, the once lucrative comedy business was experiencing a major decline. Clubs were closing throughout the country. At the same time, more and more aspiring comedians were entering the already oversaturated market. For 10 years I had had the luxury of choosing any club I wanted, at top pay. Then suddenly, gigs were getting more difficult to find and my fees were being cut nearly in half.

As the comedy industry was rapidly changing, so was my attitude about the business. It wasn't so much that I was losing my passion for stand-up comedy. In fact, I loved being onstage. I loved making people laugh. I still do. It was the business and the lifestyle that was killing me. Although I had worked hard to achieve success, it was increasingly difficult for me to actually enjoy it. Old fears and toxic labels I thought I had under control came back to haunt me.

I was partying like crazy, hoping that the booze and my comedy friends would help drown out the very loud voices in my head. Soon the evidence was piling up that things had gone too far. One time, I woke up and yelled at the dog to get out of my bed, only to realize I was in *his* bed. Another time, when I went to brush some-thing off my shoulder, it turned out to be the floor. I could go on, but I won't. Suffice it to say that my life was in a complete tailspin and it took every ounce of energy I had to fight the wrath of nega-tive thinking that attacked me.

To make this time in my life all the more intense, I kept on getting the feeling that I was being called to do something else, and I started hearing voices—well, actually my own voice—urging me to move on from the comedy scene. "This is not for you! You know you're supposed to be doing something else with your life! Now go do it."

By then, in the final years of my comedy career, I had gone on a quest to find myself and was deeply involved in the positive thought movement. I was reading dozens of self-help books, attending per-sonal development seminars, and listening to Tony Robbins CDs re-ligiously. I meditated and wrote in a journal daily.

All this activity stirred up an internal war—between me, my-self, and I; between my past and my future; between the known and unknown; and between the negative and positive forces that were battling for control. I had no idea which would prevail, but I was de-termined to find out who the real Steven Francis Rizzo was, and whether I had the courage and fortitude to allow inspiration to take me down a different path.

As all this was going on, I noticed that internal shifts were hap-pening. I was losing interest in pursuing my past desires, especially the need for fame and fortune. Slowly, I had begun to acquire a dif-ferent set of values and beliefs. Many of the things I had thought were important proved to be trivial. Auditions had become burden-some and I found that I was no longer obsessed with achieving the holy grail of comedy: my own sitcom.

Time marched on and still I tried to ignore the fact that I was going through changes. The more I suppressed my true feelings, the more chaotic and frustrating my life became. My family was on Long Island, but my work demanded that I live in Los Angeles, where I rented an apartment. When I was not on the road working to pay the bills, I was in Los Angeles, auditioning for television and radio commercials, sitcoms, and movies. In between, I would fly home and spend time with my wife, Gina, and my son, Sean.

At this juncture, my days had become about going through the motions in an angry haze. The dedication and enthusiasm I once had for my life as a comedian was virtually gone. No matter what I did or how hard I tried, my heart just wasn't in it. The fact that I was still funny, that I got consistent feedback that the "big break" was about to happen, only made me feel more miserable and confused. I had made major sacrifices, had dedicated a great part of my life to the world of stand-up comedy, and to admit to myself now that it was all over was too much to bear.

One day in the middle of a Tony Robbins seminar it hit me. This is one of the things that I love about life. You never know when or how you're going to receive that long-awaited moment of clarity. But when it hits, there is absolutely no denying it.

The lecture was over and I was putting the finishing touches on my notes. I was in awe of Tony's total command of the audience. Then I realized that what really impressed me was how he used his sense of humor as a tool to keep everyone engaged. I went to put my pen down but found that my hand still hovered over the page. I know this will sound crazy, but the pen seemed to have a mind of its own. Suddenly I (or it) began to write:

"You can do this."

"You should do this."

"You will do this."

One of the voices I referred to earlier was back, and this time the words it spoke became my wake-up call to follow my heart and pursue a career as a motivational speaker. "Yes!" I said and then wrote, "I don't know how, but that's exactly what I'm going to do. Whatever it takes."

I looked at my pen as if it had some kind of magical power and said, "Where have you been all this time?" (Then I looked over my shoulder to make sure no one was watching me, or even worse, plotting to steal my magic, life-changing Bic Roller Ball.) I told myself that the time had come for me to acknowledge the reality of my situation. Even though it was scary and confusing, I would move forward with this seemingly left-field idea and take the steps needed to make a change in my career. As soon as I came to this decision, I felt a physical surge of relief flow through my body. I knew that, somehow, I would make it work.

That's when I packed my belongings, moved out of my L.A. apartment, and flew back home to New York. A few days later, I notified my manager, agent, and publicist. I thanked them for their years of support and told them I was no longer in need of their services. They all thought I was crazy. Who could blame them? Even I thought I was crazy. But crazy or not, I had made up my mind: I was going to continue working as a comedian until my speaking career got off the ground. A career, mind you, I knew *absolutely* nothing about.

Once I surrendered and was able to make a commitment to that change, that's when things actually started to fall into place. It was as if the universe approved of my decision and began to provide the support I needed. I looked up at the heavens and said, "Okay, I'm on my way! I just wish I knew where I was going."

The uncanny thing was how often strange coincidences helped launch my speaking career. Whether it was browsing in a bookstore and randomly choosing a book with invaluable information, or meeting someone in the numerous workshops and seminars I attended, or a fortuitous conversation on a plane, people seemed to appear in my life at the exact moment I needed them. By far the most meaningful encounter I had was with the Corvette Man, a mysterious stranger I came across a few months after I flew back home to New York.

The Corvette Man

Even though I wanted to move forward with my new career, early on I had serious doubts, especially when things weren't happening as quickly as I wanted. To add to my angst, my comedy friends or former opening acts were popping up on television in commercials, sitcoms, and other new television shows. Don't get me wrong, I was happy for them. (Well, most of them, at least.) But to be honest, I was a bit jealous. I mean, every time I turned on the television, there they were at the top of their game and here I was at the very beginning stages of a new vocation. I knew I was making headway, but it just wasn't happening fast enough. I kept pushing forward, but sometimes I felt like I was banging my head against the proverbial wall. There were many moments when I thought I was losing my mind.

One such night I woke up in a cold sweat. I looked at the clock; it was 2:23 a.m. In case you're wondering, yes, that was the exact time. Some things stick with you. I got up, stumbled into the living room, and fell into the couch. My heart was racing and a rampage of negative thoughts assaulted my mind. I wanted to jump up and shout at the world, or God, or both. Hell, I just wanted to yell, and loudly.

Knowing that Gina was asleep, I reached over and grabbed a pillow, jammed my face into it, and let out a long primal scream! Tears of frustration and anger ran down my face. This went on for some time.

After a while, my body was drained. I was totally exhausted, but I felt a strange sense of inner peace. It's amazing, isn't it, how you sometimes have to go through hell to feel some peace.

I decided right then and there that I had to get some clarity and answers. I needed some kind of indisputable sign that I was on the right path. The first words out of my mouth were, "God, give me patience! Oh, and I want it now."

I smiled and felt relieved that I still had my sense of humor. I guess once a comedian, always a comedian. I continued, "I know doors have been opened, but you know me. I'm a bit neurotic and a tad insecure. I mean, look at me. Forty minutes ago I was scream-ing into a pillow. I need to know that I'm on the right path. I need to know that this is going to work, so I'm going to be very bold here and ask you for a sign. I mean a really big sign that is so obvi-ous, it simply cannot be denied. Oh, and I want it within the next 24 hours."

Later that morning, I woke up to a beautiful spring day and pro-ceeded with my usual routine—20 minutes of meditation, breakfast, and then the health club. What happened next was a turning point in my life.

As I was leaving the health club, I noticed a man in the parking lot polishing a brand-new convertible red Corvette. He was short and plump, with long brown uncombed hair, untrimmed beard, dark thick sunglasses, and a tie-dyed T-shirt. This guy looked like he should have been polishing a 1967 Volkswagen with flowers and peace signs all over it.

I don't particularly care for sports cars, especially Corvettes, but there was something about the contrast of this guy and that auto-mobile that made me laugh.

Trying not to show my amusement, I walked over and said, "Nice car."

"Thanks," he said. "But they're hard to keep clean." He moved over to the front of the car to buff the headlight covers. It was then that I noticed the license plate read COMEDY and featured a handicap symbol next to it. Now he really had my attention.

"Are you a comedian?" I asked.

"No."

"Why do you have 'comedy' on your license plate?" I pursued.

"Because I always wanted to be a comedian," he explained. "People need to laugh, especially today. I think our sense of humor is one of the greatest gifts God ever gave us. I would like to be a giver of that gift."

I started to tell him that I was a comedian, but he interrupted me and said, "Excuse me, I'm not finished yet." He continued, "People need to know that they're okay. Humor can help them through the tough times. Humor brings hope. Anyone who has the ability to convey that message, make people laugh, or feel good in any way is truly blessed."

I just stood there listening to this guy who looked like a refugee from the 1960s as he buffed his car. He stopped, put down the rag, looked at me, and said, "I saw you on TV. Steve Rizzo, right?"

I nodded.

"You're very funny," he said, smiling. "Do you want to know why I have the handicap sign on my license plate?"

"Yeah. Why?"

"From carrying too much weight," he said. "Instead of carrying a little at a time, I tried to carry the whole load at once. You're bound to hurt yourself when you do that." He picked up his rag and continued to buff his car.

I was about to ask him what he was trying to carry when he interrupted me again. "People do that a lot, you know. They set goals, have dreams, and instead of enjoying the process, they expect immediate results, instant gratification, and a guarantee that they're doing the right thing. And when things don't go the way they want or as fast as they want, they panic and leave themselves open to fear and other negative emotions."

He paused, shook his head, and looked right at me and said, "That type of thinking is bound to weigh them down. It's too much of a load for anyone to carry." He paused a long moment, then continued, "You know, there really aren't any shortcuts to success and happiness. There are no guarantees. Only choices. Choices and faith. You should always choose to follow your heart."

I didn't say a word. I couldn't say a word. I just listened and watched as he shined his car. Then he leaned back against the fender, crossed his arms, contemplated a bit, and said, "Do you want to know what one of the keys for fulfilling a dream is?"

Again, I couldn't say anything, but to myself I thought, "Oh shit, here we go again!"

"Take one step at a time," he said, "because the steps are the journey and with each step is an experience to encounter, a lesson to learn. You need them in order to truly embrace the fulfillment of the dream. To appreciate what you have is to appreciate how you earned it." He laughed and said, "Hey, that's heavy. I should be a philosopher."

He put down the rag and walked up to me. I couldn't see his eyes through his sunglasses, but I knew he was looking directly into mine. I was speechless. I knew exactly what had just transpired. The only words that came out of my mouth were, "Thank you."

He smiled and said, "It was wonderful talking with you." He reached out both of his hands, firmly held mine, and said, "God bless you, Steve. You have a wonderful gift. Use it. Use it, and share your humor and your message with the world."

Many people with whom I share this story believe this mysterious man was an angel. It's not my purpose, however, to prove the existence of angels or angelic happenings. That's Sylvia Browne's job. The point is that someone I had never met before answered my prayer within hours after I prayed. This proves, at least to me, that there is something greater out there beyond our existence. It also made me think that if God did send me this particular angel, then surely God must have a sense of humor.

What is an angel anyway but a messenger? What's the difference if my mysterious hippie friend was a messenger with supernatural powers or someone from FedEx? What mattered is that this stranger delivered a very personal message to me that enabled me to move on with my life with faith and hope. My prayer had been answered.

Following the encounter with the Corvette Man, a massive flow of information came my way. Unlikely situations and incredible opportunities continued to confirm that I was on the right path. And that path became my mission, my yellow brick road.

Throughout my travels as a speaker/comedian and personal development trainer, events have led me to people who have overcome major challenges in their lives, from financial disaster to the loss of a loved one. Some were seriously injured in an accident; others were diagnosed with cancer or infected with HIV. In all cases, these people proclaimed that their ability to shift their focus from the negative to the positive was the key factor in either a full recovery or a total acceptance of their situation that allowed them peace of mind. Thus the title of the book, *Get Your SHIFT Together.*

Through my own and other people's stories I will reveal how the power of shifting your focus and way of thinking can affect your perception of challenging circumstances and even life's tragedies, literally training yourself to become a happier, more confident, and successful person, on all levels of life.

Ironically, other people's stories paved the way toward my own healing. And believe me, I needed healing.

Motivate This

2

> The biggest mistake a person
> can make is to be afraid of
> making one.
>
> **ELBERT HUBBARD**

L et's take a trip down memory lane to my college days at a time when I was a leading actor in Samuel Beckett's *Waiting for Godot*, a play that falls into the category of what theater aficionados call Theater of the Absurd.

All three acts of the play are about the interaction between two homeless people, Estragon (played by yours truly) and Vladimir. These two lost souls meet every day at the same place for the sole purpose of waiting for another character named Godot, who will tell them what to do with their lives. Godot, you see, has all the answers. He will show them the way to success and happiness.

Through the characters Beckett comically and yet tragically shows how we get trapped in our own inertia and eventually become self-proclaimed card-carrying victims of society. The tragedy is not that Godot never comes. We don't even know if Godot exists. The real tragedy is that Estragon and Vladimir wait day after day, year after year, as time ticks away and life passes them by. They never take the initiative to help themselves. They do nothing to change their unproductive circumstances. Yet every day they expect something to happen. I've heard insanity defined as doing things the way you've always done them but expecting a different outcome. These two characters in *Waiting for Godot* are the epitome of such behavior.

I won an award for best actor and received high praise from the critics that year for the role of Estragon. I'm not telling you this to impress you, but to impress upon you that the reason I did such a "scrupulous job," as one critic wrote, was because I wasn't acting. I *was* Estragon. I related to his plight.

As a child, I acquired many fears and limiting beliefs about myself and the world that surrounded me. For a great part of my life I believed that circumstances determined my fate. I didn't understand that I could have chosen a better way. My experiences with adults, teachers, and my peers led me to believe that I simply wasn't good enough or smart enough. After being saddled with the dubious high school honor of "Least Likely to Succeed," after being told by a guidance counselor that I didn't have the intelligence to make it through college, I wore the label "loser" with a certain amount of twisted pride.

But years of feeling inadequate, of habitual negative thinking, eventually created labels that led me to believe that dreams were the luxury of only a fortunate few, and I wasn't one of them. Like Estragon and Vladimir, I woke up every morning waiting for my life to happen. If anyone needed an attitude adjustment, it was me.

The real danger set in when I left home and tried to make it on my own. Looking back at my comedy career, I can see how and why I sabotaged so many opportunities. Unaware, I carried with me many of my unresolved negative labels and limiting beliefs. As a result, I kept reliving the same mistakes and failures over and over again. I knew I had the talent, but I couldn't understand why I wasn't getting my big break. My perceived limitations had me confused, and my fears paralyzed me. In fact, I figured out that I had a fear of failure *and* a fear of success. (Talk about not being able to make up your mind!) Sounds crazy, but I never said I was normal.

At the time, I didn't know that fear of failure and success were normal feelings, experienced by almost everyone at one time or another. At the time, I didn't know I had options on how to respond or that I could have created a healthier belief system simply by consistently shifting my focus and way of thinking. I honestly was clueless to what I know now—you empower yourself when you feel the fear and move forward anyway. Instead I allowed fear to use me. Finally, however, I was able to realize that opportunity had been knocking all along, I was just afraid to open the door. I was allowing the toxic labels that had been thrust upon me to dictate the story of my life.

Four years after high school, I finally mustered up enough courage to go to college. I went on to surprise everyone, including myself, by excelling with honors at the university and postgraduate levels. College was not always easy for me. There were many times when my toxic labels ("Danger! Failure Ahead!") came back to haunt me, but I always somehow managed to bounce back and persevere. Eventually, I got a job teaching at my old high school, proving once and for all that guidance counselors are not fortune-tellers.

The most valuable lesson I've learned is that nothing in life is wasted if I view it as a lesson learned. I now understand that every step I took, whether forward or backward, was necessary to prepare me to recognize and receive whatever gift was being given to me at the time. I needed every experience to help me grow. And I mean *every single* experience: the good and the bad, the successes and the failures, the pain and the glory. As a result of these myriad experiences, I have earned the credibility to do what I do today, which is to help people learn to be happy and successful no matter what their circumstances.

My quest to overcome the obstacles that were keeping me from the life I truly desired has brought my work full circle. I am truly grateful that I've come to the understanding that I never quit stand-up comedy. I simply let go and yielded to a greater purpose. A new dream. Okay, I didn't simply let go. At times I held on with white knuckles in a desperate grip, kicking and screaming! The point is, when I finally did let go, I was free to pursue my true dream—to use humor and the power of positive thinking to help teach people to learn the skills they need to get to a better place at work and in life.

I'm here to show you how to knock down emotional barriers, how to develop healthy, rock-solid mental habits and create the foundation of hope and optimism you need to have a happy life. I will also provide you with commonsense techniques to solve problems and humorous strategies on how to bounce back from stressful situations.

I'm here to tell you that no matter what your given circumstances, you can adjust your attitude and create a brighter reality. It's not the bad neighborhood you grew up in that led you on the wrong path. It's not the teacher who shunned your artistic talents or the parent who suggested you weren't good enough that caused you to become stagnant. And it's not the illness you have or the accident that left you physically challenged that's keeping you in a state of isolation.

I'm in no way trying to trivialize life's tribulations. Let's face it: some of us have a great deal of pain to deal with. However, it is essential for your well-being that you understand that circumstances, events, or situations are not the final word on your quality of life, no matter the severity. It's how you respond to them and the fear and other negative emotions they elicit that makes the difference. And more than anything it's about making the mental shift in attitude that will allow you to power through whatever life throws at you. In fact, it's all about attitude. It's always been about attitude. And always *will* be about attitude.

You know what kind of attitude I'm talking about? A New York attitude. Don't give me that look! I'm serious. New Yorkers have always had a reputation for dealing with adversity of any kind. No matter the severity of the situation, New Yorkers not only bounce back, they thrive with steadfast determination and confidence that defy the odds against them.

Do you want to know how to acquire a New York attitude? All you have to do is observe a cat, any cat. In my view, cats by their very nature exemplify the New York attitude. There you go giving me that look again. Go ahead. Just watch them. They strut around the house as if they're God's gift to the animal kingdom. I swear, if cats could talk we would hear, "Meow! Meow! Ba-da-bing! Meow!"

Why is it said that cats have nine lives? Because they have resilience, they bounce back. Nothing seems to affect these animals. I once saw a cat run full force smack into a wall, bounce off, land on its feet, and look at me as if to say, "What? I knew it was there! I meant to do that!" and then walk away. "Ba-da-bing! Meow!"

Have you ever told a cat to go fetch something? It just sits there and gives you another one of those looks. "Hey, let's get something straight. I don't do fetch. You want something, you tell your best friend Rover to get it. I'm busy. I've got company comin' over. And when they get here, don't embarrass me with this 'Here Kitty, Kitty' crap. I got a name! You use it! Even if it is Fluffy! You use it!"

The bottom line: cats live on their own terms. Nobody tells them what to do. They defy the odds. And they bounce back and have resilience. I'll say it again: cats have a New York attitude! And all of us can use some of that!

A perfect example of someone who has always had a New York attitude is my older brother Michael.

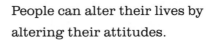

The Finger of Optimism

People can alter their lives by
altering their attitudes.

WILLIAM JAMES

The biggest inspiration in my life is my brother Michael. No one taught me how to confront fear and to be optimistic through adverse times better than him. He is 100 percent disabled as a result of the Vietnam War. Twenty-one feet of his small intestine was either blown out on the battlefield or removed on the operating table. He also had damage to his large intestine, kidneys, and other internal organs. Sorry to be so graphic, but I want you to fully appreciate his condition so you can understand the significance of what he overcame.

According to experts, Michael is the only person in medical history to survive that kind of injury. Actually, he's doing more than surviving. He's living a full life. Michael is married, has two children, and has recently retired as assistant superintendent of schools for a district on Long Island, New York. This guy has more energy and enthusiasm than anyone I know. If you were to see him today you would never know what he went through.

I remember the first time I saw him after he came home. He was at St. Albans Naval Hospital in Queens. If my mom and dad hadn't been in the room when I entered, I never would have known it was my own brother lying there. He had gone from 170 pounds of Marine muscle to 88 pounds of skin and bone. At the end of the day a doctor entered the room, approached my parents, and said, "I'm sorry, but it doesn't look promising at all." I'll never forget the look on my parents' faces or the sight of two of Michael's friends from high school walking out the hospital room door. The doctor continued, "It would be a miracle for him or anyone to survive such an ordeal." His Marine Corps buddy was hitting the wall, repeatedly demanding of no one in particular, "Why?"

As all of this was happening, I remember staring at my brother and wondering if that was going to be the last time I would ever see him. Then I noticed something strange. His hand was slowly rising from his side. He was aware of what was going on. He must have heard the doctor's prognosis, because he slowly clenched his fist, and to my surprise, his middle finger popped straight out. I remember saying, "That's no muscle spasm!"

Luckily for that doctor, the raising of the middle finger replaced the words Michael was unable to verbalize. It became his declaration to the entire world that he was not going to give up on his life—that he would more than survive, he would flourish. Counter to its generally accepted meaning, that extended finger was a symbol of hope and Michael's personally customized salute to recovery. It represented his opinion of that doctor's prognosis and it was the answer that he gave all of the doctors every time they told him what he could or couldn't do. He found great joy in proving them wrong.

We now refer to this gesture as "the finger of optimism" (or "up-timism," as I put it). I knew without a doubt, from the raising of that finger, that the spirit that resided in Michael John Rizzo was still alive. His sense of humor was intact and he clearly had his wits about him. Somehow, he was going to try and make it.

One day, a group of doctors told him that because of his unique condition he would need to adhere to a special lifelong diet consisting primarily of oatmeal, soups, fruit, baby food, and juice. I mean, let's face it, they were talking about someone who had only one foot of small intestine. Every time he swallowed something he had difficulty retaining it. But my brother defiantly looked at the doctors and said, "No way! You will not tell me what I can and cannot do! I'm going to eat a bowl of pasta and a couple of meatballs, even if I have to sit on the toilet while I do it!"

Another time, he was being reprimanded by a doctor for eating a sandwich. My brother looked at the doctor and said, "The difference between you and me, Doc, is that you keep concentrating on the 21 feet of intestine I lost. And I keep concentrating on the 1 foot I still have. Let's see what I can do with that." Then he belched and said, "Now, what's for dessert?"

Bear in mind that Michael was in a ward filled with young men who were suffering physically, mentally, emotionally, and spiritually. He witnessed bodies being brought in and out for close to a year. Every day he heard their cries. He felt their pain. At times it must have been unbearable.

The many long, dark nights in the hospital provided plenty of opportunity for Michael to consider how unlucky and unfair a situation he was in, but I never once heard him utter so much as a "Why me?" He never blamed the war, the Marine Corps, or his country. Surrounded by chaos and having to deal with his own plight, he was still able to harness enough energy to shift his focus onto what needed to be done to get himself out of there and what he was going to do once he did. In other words, through training himself to use the power of shifting, Michael literally created his own miracle, even when the odds were dead set against him.

It was this type of attitude that allowed Michael to find and navigate the road to recovery. When he finally was able to speak, the only words he allowed himself were those that served to build his self-esteem. And in time he was able to adapt to his new digestive system. Doctors still don't know how he does it, but he eats anything he wants and fully enjoys it.

Amazingly, Michael's confidence was a stabilizing force for those around him. The family fed off of his positive attitude, and even in the face of wave after wave of discouraging news, everyone's spirits rose along with his health. It's funny now to think that the most contagious thing at St. Albans during that period was Michael's powerfully positive attitude. "I'm still Mike Rizzo," he would say, and he would launch into a detailed description of what he was going to do once he was released from the hospital.

I swear there were times when he seemed to relish the challenge. He found great joy in proving the experts wrong. Every diagnosis he foiled put another notch on his victory belt and another step toward his full recovery.

Do you see the mindset he created? Do you understand how his viewpoint and choice of words created an empowering belief system that helped him to feel confident, even in a situation that took his mortality for granted? Can you see how this type of attitude can affect your present and future reality?

Some people say that my brother's life and the way he lives it today fall nothing short of miraculous. I agree completely. I believe in miracles. I believe in divine intervention. I also believe that when times are tough, especially when the odds are against us, we all have opportunities to perform our own miracles. It's a matter of how you perceive and meet the challenge. And sometimes, we just need that one finger.

I believe without a doubt that Michael's greatest weapon in his fight for survival was his steadfast determination to shift away from the negative forces that might consume him toward a positive, healthier mindset. He has an uncanny ability to shift his focus and way of thinking to instantly change how he views a challenging situation. This change in perception always gives him the hope, confidence, and courage he needs to move forward. You can definitely say my brother has his shift together.

Another key concept that helped my brother meet the challenge of his recovery is that he never put his happiness on hold. Many of the wounded in that hospital created and held on to the belief that they couldn't be happy with their current situation, or at best, that they would only begin to enjoy their lives if and when they had a full recovery. Michael took a different stance and strove to enjoy himself and find the laughter during the rebuilding process.

I am not by any means trying to insinuate that he did not have his bad days. At times his situation seemed hopeless. But he knew he couldn't allow himself to be taken over by negative forces. When he felt he was going down, he would build himself up with words of encouragement. Yes, he knew that his life would never be the same. But in spite of that reality, he was able to choose to shift his focus to things that lifted his spirits. He insisted on surrounding himself with people who were optimistic and had a sense of humor.

This is where family and friends were able to make a big difference. We would often tell funny stories about growing up and crack jokes about hospital procedures. One of the best was when I took a rubber surgical glove and blew it up like a balloon. Once the five fingers were inflated, I went down on all fours, put the balloon under my stomach, and started mooing and talking like a cow with a New York attitude. When the head nurse came by I said, "Excuse me. Can you tell me where I'm supposed to go for my Udder-O-Gram?" You had to be there, but trust me when I say it cracked everyone up.

A patient two beds away from my brother was laughing hard and screaming for a bedpan at the same time. Unfortunately, the bedpan didn't get there in time. That's when the nurse who was trying to keep it together by being stern escorted me to a chair and said sternly, "You know we have a psychiatric ward in this hospital for people like you."

Laughter not only helped to boost my brother's morale, but that of the other patients surrounding him.

To Michael, it was never the end of the world; rather, it was the beginning of a new one. He viewed his situation as a challenge, not a catastrophe. Even the slightest accomplishment, like getting out of bed to walk to the bathroom without assistance, was a victory. Each victory brought more stability to his foundation of hope. Hope strengthened his conviction to be grateful for what he had. The more grateful he was, the more he tried to accomplish, and before long he had created his own perpetual cycle, a whirlwind of positive energy that propelled him to achieve far more than anyone would have predicted. His gusto for life was extraordinary and still is.

When Michael was released from the hospital he weighed 95 pounds. We were all surprised when he declared that he was going to go to college and become a history teacher. To be honest, we had our doubts. Not only would his physical condition be an obstacle, but Michael wasn't exactly Mr. Whiz Kid in high school. We're talking about a guy who had no academic or vocational skills at all.

Once again Michael beat the odds. He graduated college with high honors and received degrees in history, education, and administration. After graduating, he landed a job as a history teacher at the same high school he graduated from. After a few years he was appointed the school's attendance officer. Not too long after that he became assistant principal. He had the respect not only of the faculty, but of the students and parents as well. It was no surprise, then, when he was offered and accepted the position of principal of the local middle school.

Wait! There's more! When Michael was seriously contemplating retirement, the powers that be asked him to consider taking on the job of assistant superintendent of the entire school district, which of course he did. It was the perfect ending for a wonderful career.

Michael is now retired and traveling the world with his wife, Joan. In the summer he spends much of his time at his beautiful home in upstate New York. During the winter months he resides in his condominium in Florida. Not bad for someone who was told he would never make it out of the hospital alive. Michael's experience proves to me without a shadow of a doubt that with the right attitude, even with only one foot of intestine, all you have to do is put one foot in front of the other.

Michael's story is proof that it's not what happens to us that determines our fate, but rather what we do about what happens that makes the difference. It's the choices we make and the actions we take along the way; it's the thoughts we have; what we focus on and how we frame what we tell ourselves 24/7. It's about making a rock-solid commitment to enjoy ourselves during the rebuilding process, and to dare to find the laughter during the tough times.

Now you know why Michael is the biggest inspiration in my life. The lessons I learned from him during his recovery and through the years have been invaluable. Seeing his remarkable ability to shift his mindset is without a doubt the catalyst that allowed me to turn my own life around and the inspiration for my career.

Too many of us relinquish control of our lives and accept our circumstances for what they might seem to be. We don't know we have a choice, the tools, the power, or the know-how to confront our fears and challenges head-on. Practicing the attitude-shifting strategies outlined in this book will enable you to build healthy mental habits that will help break down walls of negativity and give you a brighter perspective on all aspects of life. This shift in attitude and belief will transform the labels holding you back to ones that will propel you forward with confidence.

If you've had enough struggles, if your life is lacking in some meaningful way, continue reading, my friend. It is my wish that the insights I deliver will help you to build bridges to a better future. I am confident that the stories and methods I offer here will stimulate the spark of hope and creativity that will allow you to implement the simple, internal solutions to turn your life around.

Your life isn't predestined for greatness. Nor is it predestined for failure. It's up to you to create a belief system that allows you to see your life from a position of advantage rather than disadvantage, from a position of a field general surveying the overall battle plan rather than living and dying with every small infantry misstep. Only you can choose to shift your focus during adverse times. Only you can choose to shift your thoughts and words to turn challenges into opportunities. Believe me when I say that talent and ability are not the only factors that determine a successful and happy life.

For your sake, especially during tough times, get into the habit of choosing positive thoughts and speaking empowering words. Focus on hope, gratitude, and seeing the good during adverse times, and you will discover a brighter day, regardless of what is happening to you.

To help you, I have organized the balance of this book in three more parts that will occasionally address what I call my Attitude Adjustment Strategies, which will help you become a natural at shifting your attitude.

In Part 2, I will show you the importance of enjoying yourself during the process of whatever you're trying to achieve. Learn how to start each day with an unstoppable attitude that will help elevate your degree of overall happiness. In other words, you can be happier than you ever thought possible. I will show you how.

In Part 3, you will learn that it's not necessarily what happens to you that determines your quality of success and happiness, but rather how you think about what happens. I will also show how and why humor nips negative thoughts in the bud, before they wreak emotional havoc.

In Part 4, you will notice how awareness, common sense, and a sense of humor can change your perception of what I've identified as the two major imposing forces: fear and the Big Mouth inside your head.

Practice and own the strategies within each part and you will realize how much power you have over every aspect of your life. You can turn your life around. You can change your way of being. You can experience your challenges from a healthier perspective. You can create wealth and prosperity. You can enjoy yourself during the process of whatever you are trying to achieve. You can laugh off your fears. You can be happier than you ever imagined. You can choose a better way to live.

Once you realize that your daily reality is a mirror of the thoughts you have and the actions you take, then change in any area of your life is possible and, what's more, well within your control. By shifting your focus, thoughts, words, and beliefs, you can change what's happening around you and change your world.

Remember, the only losers in the game of life are those who, for whatever reason, fail to use their challenges as a springboard for growth.

So are you ready to get your shift together? If not, then you better shift and get off the pot, because when shift happens, your life changes. At this point you've probably had enough of my shift. I guess you can say I'm full of shift. I apologize; sometimes I'm just a real shifthead. Oh shift, I did it again!

Seriously folks: may the shift be with you.

Part 2

Shift into a Happier Mindset

There are as many nights as days, and the one is just as long as the other in the year's course. Even a happy life cannot be without a measure of darkness, and the word "happy" would lose its meaning if it were not balanced by sadness.

CARL JUNG

The first thing I want you to understand is the importance of making a conscious choice to enjoy yourself during the process of whatever you are trying to achieve. Making happiness a choice is what it's all about. No matter what your personal or professional circumstances, you can adjust your attitude and elevate your degree of overall happiness by choosing to shift your present mindset. When you fully appreciate that the mood you're in right this second affects how you'll deal with what's coming next, you will want to make the choices that will help you to feel better, not worse. That, my friend, is a major key to living a successful, happy life.

Remember, when shift happens, your life changes.

Enjoy the Process

4

> If we agree that the bottom line is happiness, not success, then it makes perfect sense to say that it is the journey that counts, not reaching the destination.
>
> **MIHALY CSIKSZENTMIHALYI**

Many of my clients refer to me as "the Attitude Adjuster." Why? I help people realize how they can acquire the attitude they need to succeed in all levels of life while enjoying the process. Therein lies the key, my friend: "while enjoying the process." Unfortunately, in this day and age, enjoyment seems to be something that many people leave by the wayside, especially when change is taking place and the pressure is on to reinvent yourself and achieve new goals, or when there are tight deadlines to be met and things aren't going exactly as planned. Now more than ever, people are having difficulty balancing their lives, and there just doesn't seem to be enough time to get everything done. This is when the stress levels become overwhelming and self-doubt, anger, uncertainty, fear, and a host of other negative emotions can create a dangerous mindset. Without realizing it, people deny themselves enjoyment and lose their ability to laugh and have fun at the time when it's most crucial.

Studies have shown that those who make conscious choices to enjoy themselves and laugh throughout the day are more creative, productive, and resilient to challenging situations. They are also more likely to easily find solutions to complex problems. In other words, focusing on your happiness makes you smarter. How smart are you?

"Intellectual benefits of a good laugh," says Daniel Goleman, author of *Emotional Intelligence*, "are most striking when it comes to solving problems that demand a creative solution."

In a study testing creative thinking, experts found that the participants' ability to solve a puzzle was positively affected by their ability to take a humorous approach to the task. In the test, groups of people are given a candle, matches, and a box of tacks. They are asked to attach the candle to a corkboard wall so that it burns without dripping wax onto the floor.

"Given the challenge, most people fall into 'functional fixedness,'" says Goleman. "They think about using the objects in the most conventional ways. But people who have just watched a funny film, compared to people who have watched a film about math or who have exercised, were more likely to see an alternative use for the box holding the tacks. They come up with the creative solution of tacking the box to the wall and using it as a candle holder."

A study done at San Diego State University followed students who thoroughly enjoyed themselves as they attended a series of lectures that contained humor and funny anecdotes. These students achieved higher test scores than students who attended the same lectures but without the humorous elements. Why? Because they were enjoying the process.

When I speak to groups I usually ask for a show of hands of how many people get upset when they're stuck in traffic. Without fail, mostly everyone will raise their hand. Then I suggest that instead of letting a traffic jam make them crazy, they laugh it off.

At this point about half the audience gives me a look as if I have absolutely no idea what I'm talking about. Consider this: most people would agree that your mood can affect your quality of happiness and success. So, taking the example of a traffic jam, if you understand that the mood a traffic jam puts you in can determine your mood for the rest of the day, what would you rather choose to do? Work yourself up into a frenzy over something you have no control over or laugh it off?

What if later in the day you have a business meeting scheduled with a challenging client or a situation arises at work that requires your full attention? Or maybe it's your anniversary and you have a special dinner planned with your spouse or it's your child's birthday and the party is just a couple hours away. The point is that your mood, good or bad, has an incredible power to affect the outcome of everything you do. So instead of getting angry, why not make an attempt to enjoy yourself and laugh when you're in traffic? The same goes for when you're feeling stressed about your workload or at times when everyone seems to be getting on your nerves. Why not choose to enjoy the day, even when things aren't going the way you want? Why not allow yourself to laugh at life's mishaps and absurdities?

When I'm stuck in traffic or in any other stressful situation I understand that I have a choice. I can either let the situation control my emotions or I can adjust my attitude and take control. Experience has taught me that certain choices will not only keep me from enjoying the day, but will hinder my ability to deal productively with whatever requires my attention. Because I'm aware of these repercussions, I will do anything in my power to keep myself from letting a bad mood overtake me.

Here's a personal example. Oftentimes when I'm in the midst of a stressful situation I vent my frustrations in the voice of a famous person or cartoon character. You might call me crazy, but since I'm good at and enjoy doing impressions, the result is that the tension dissipates, my mood changes, and I'm able to find enjoyment in the moment and bounce back. It doesn't matter if I'm alone or with others, it works every time.

One evening, after a 12-hour rehearsal, I was driving home from the city anticipating a relaxing evening at home. I was in a great mood, having just spent the day playing the Cowardly Lion in a business parody of *The Wizard of Oz*. But as John Lennon once said, "Life is what happens to you while you're busy making other plans."

There was construction on the Long Island Expressway, otherwise known as the World's Biggest Parking Lot. It would be hours before I would reach my long-awaited destination. The probability of spending quality time at home with my wife was not in my favor. My good mood was fading fast and my frustration was slowly but surely turning into anger. Now, I don't know what came over me, but suddenly I had the urge to vent and began shouting out obscenities in the voice of the Cowardly Lion. The thought of the Lion swearing like a truck driver made me laugh.

Traffic was at a complete standstill and it was obvious that people were getting agitated. To make matters worse, some of the drivers were moving onto the shoulder of the road and then trying to conveniently force their way back in line. This is something New Yorkers don't take lightly. Tempers were flaring, horns were sounding, and people were cursing and making all kinds of hand gestures. As all of this is taking place, I'm behind the wheel of my car, motioning to the other drivers (as the Cowardly Lion). "Grrah, grraha, aha, aha, ahaaaa, I'm afraid! I wanna go home! I wanna go home! Everybody is cutting ahead! I don't like traffic. I wanna go home! Ahaa, ahaa, haa!"

Humor is subjective, and you may not find this funny, but if you had seen the expressions on the faces of those I passed I guarantee you would have laughed. I could only imagine what they were thinking or saying. "Don't look at him, honey!" "Lock the door and look straight ahead!" "What's wrong with that guy? No, don't look at him. He's not right!" "I'll bet he's some kind of pervert. He's probably naked from the waist down!" "Please! Just look straight ahead and keep driving!"

While you might think I'm nuts, and anyone witnessing my crazy antics might agree, at least I know I will be going home to my family or to a client meeting or making an important decision in a *good* mood. In fact, my energy level is cranked. Why? Because I am able to change my state of mind. I'm actually going from a bad mood to a good one, just by choosing to make a slight shift to see the humor in a tough situation and allowing myself the freedom to laugh. Choosing to defuse a stressful situation with humor is just one way to acquire the attitude you need to succeed while enjoying the process. As you will see throughout this book, making this choice is very empowering.

What truly amazes me is that there are those who actually believe that if you are enjoying yourself and having fun at work, you're simply not doing your job properly. That's a lot of bull poop! The fact is—and you can prove this to yourself at any time—if you're having fun at work everyone benefits. This holds true for every aspect of our lives. No matter who you are or what you're doing, whether you're teaching or learning, if you are enjoying the process the odds are in your favor that you'll achieve the outcome you desire. It seems obvious to consciously choose happiness, but I would wager any amount of money that when writing out their short- or long-term goals and plans, most people don't count enjoying themselves during the process as part of the equation.

Let me quickly define for you what I mean when I refer to "the process." It's not just the steps you take in a direct effort to achieve a particular goal, but is your life in its entirety. This means all daily activities that make up your life—whether picking up your dry cleaning, feeding the baby, or taking a nap. In other words, "the process" is your life.

"If choosing happiness is such an obvious thing to do," you may ask, "then why is it so darn hard to remember to do it consistently?" This is a fair question, and the answer may surprise you. It turns out that your receding hairline or thick ankles aren't the only things you can blame on your ancestors.

Daniel Gilbert, author of *Stumbling on Happiness*, reasons that the human evolutionary process itself may cause our tendency to overlook happiness in any given moment. Our early ancestors were constantly seeking a safer environment, more food, and better shelter. It was a matter of survival. That kind of doggedness was necessary for cavemen. On some level, however, we've allowed "If only I had a bigger cave" to become the mantra of our species. Therefore we must be diligent and remind ourselves that our constant pressure to achieve our professional and personal goals is no reason not to enjoy the steps along the way.

Unfortunately, we hung on to the leopard-print leotards as well. The workout crazes of the early 1980s brought about the phrase "No pain, no gain," and American culture was quick to adopt it in every facet of life. In 2005, David Morris wrote in the *Scientist* magazine, "'No pain, no gain' is an American modern mini-narrative: it compresses the story of a protagonist who understands that the road to achievement runs only through hardship." The perception was and continues to be that if you're having fun you must not be getting anything worthwhile done. I'll say it again, and this time I'll bypass the poop. That's bullshit! Don't get me wrong. I'm not advocating that everyone sit around all day being content with what they have. I'm suggesting that not only is it okay, but it's your right to enjoy every step you take toward achieving your goals. If you are consistently making choices to enjoy yourself during the process of whatever it is that you are trying to achieve, you will more than likely get there easier and faster.

I am constantly amazed by the ways that people manage to deny themselves the chance at happiness in the moment. Instead, they fall prey to a dangerous mindset that decreases their potential for happiness. They put their happiness on hold when they repeat and internalize negative statements like, "When I finally buy a house, I'll be less stressed and I can enjoy myself," or "I'll be happy when I'm able to retire," or "I would be happy if I only made more money."

Trust me when I say there are always more bills to pay and something expensive to repair around the house. Unexpected setbacks will occur and new work projects will quickly replace the ones that are currently stressing you out. Statements that focus on what you lack in the present, or predicate happiness on a future event, destroy your chance of enjoying the moment.

The good news is that there are always fresh opportunities to be happy. Imagine life is like Grand Central Station where happy times arrive around the clock. Chances are, the opportunity to be happy has already arrived. Sometimes it's right in front of you. For whatever reason, you are unable to shift your focus to notice and appreciate it. Regardless of what is going on around you, you can feel happier, you can be productive, attract success, and enjoy yourself during the process. When you shift your focus and the way you think, your perspective changes. When shift happens, your life changes. So get your shift together.

Let's say Bernie is having a difficult time enjoying his day. I don't know Bernie and I don't even know what he does for a living. It really doesn't matter because he's someone I've made up to make my point. But, hey, if your name happens to be Bernie, *wow*! What were the chances you were going to be used as an example when you picked up this book? Well, 100 percent, I guess, but you didn't know that, did you? See? Anything is possible.

So Bernie is having a tough time enjoying the day. His mind is reeling with all sorts of complaints and negative self-talk. "Right now, there are just too many things happening in my life. There are too many changes taking place. My job is absolutely driving me out of my mind. I just learned how to work that stupid software and now they're telling me that I have to learn a whole different system. Why can't they make up their minds? I'll tell you why! Because nobody cares about my needs, that's why! I am not appreciated and I certainly don't get the respect I deserve! When things calm down and my life starts working the way I want, then I'll allow myself to enjoy things."

I think it's fair to say that Bernie needs an attitude adjustment. Let me explain what you (or Bernie) are doing to yourself when you think this way. You are literally putting your happiness on hold. You are convincing yourself that the happiness you deserve now is dependent on something that has to take place in the future. That is insane! It's also natural, so don't go admitting yourself into a mental institution just yet. All the same, you have to take positive steps to reverse that human instinct to withhold happiness from yourself, or else your ability to enjoy life will always be at least one step ahead of you.

For some people, it seems a virtue to defer happiness and enjoyment. I'm reminded of the phrase, "All good things come to those who wait." Let's discuss this nugget of wisdom, shall we? Granted, patience is a virtue. I understand that more often than not we have to wait to reap the fruits of our labor. But not at the expense of being happy! This phrase implies that you have to wait for happiness, that the end result is the only place where happiness resides. It completely ignores the fact that enjoyment can be experienced during the process. Hey folks, it takes a long time for fruit to grow. Why not pick a few wild berries while you wait?

There are far too many people holding on to their precious ticket to Happy Land, waiting for the Good Time Express to arrive. Give me a break! Better yet, give yourself a break. This defies all logic. Why wait for good times? Why not have them now? In fact, now is the only place where good times can happen. They can't happen in the past and they can't happen in the future.

The point I'm making is that happiness can only be experienced in the present, in the moment of whatever it is that you are trying to achieve right now. There is absolutely no reason why you can't plan for the future, set goals, go through your daily routine, deal with the unexpected, and still make conscious choices to enjoy yourself while doing so. People who consistently enjoy the process not only reap the benefits of achieving their goal, but they also have a fond appreciation of how they earned it. In my view that is the ultimate success.

Whether you're at home cleaning out the garage, making cold sales calls, comparing prices of brands of peanut butter, or preparing a pitch to win more business for your company, it is your right to enjoy yourself. That may be one of the keys to attaining happiness: understanding that happiness is your personal right, just like freedom of speech and being able to vote. It's curious to me that we have laws in place to make sure no one infringes upon our right to happiness, yet we are so often a willing impediment to our own enjoyment of life. The U.S. Constitution guarantees the right to "the pursuit of happiness." Maybe it should read "life, liberty, and the happiness of the pursuit."

You might be thinking, "So what if I have to wait to get what I want to be happy? Aren't some things worth waiting for?" It's true that some things are worth waiting for—the caramel at the bottom of an ice cream sundae comes to mind. But certainly not your happiness. You can't wait for happiness. Of course you feel happy once you get what you want. You've completed the task and received your due reward. Life is good again. You can relax and enjoy yourself for the rest of time, right?

Sorry to break it to you, but happiness doesn't work that way. What you're really experiencing is not happiness, but temporary relief. Relief is fine. It's certainly a by-product of happiness, which is welcome and feels good, but it's not long-lasting and it's not true happiness. In a short time you will notice the return of that same needful, longing mindset, and the elation, brought on by attaining your heart's desire, starts to recede. It's at this point that the cycle begins again, making your attainment of happiness into a carrot to trudge after. You can find yourself thinking, "Okay. That was nice. I achieved that goal and I have all the money I want. But for some reason the thrill is gone. Now, what else do I have to achieve so that I can be happy once again?" When you convince yourself that your happiness is dependent upon something that has to take place in the future, it is difficult to enjoy the present. Let me blow your mind for a moment: the present is a gift. Unwrap it.

In all my years of being a stand-up comedian, I've known many comics who put their happiness on hold. They had difficulty enjoying the process because they believed they wouldn't be happy until they signed with HBO, got their own sitcom or movie deal, or whatever it was they thought would make them happy. I know, because I was one of them.

Over the years I've seen close friends morph into bitter, jealous, and resentful people who no longer enjoyed making people laugh. Without ever realizing what they were doing to themselves, they got caught up in their own quest to become a star, which in their minds was the only thing that would make them happy. The world of show business became their only business. Their whole existence revolved around getting "discovered," which was ironic because they had no idea how lost they really were. It was disheartening to see that they never allowed themselves the time to appreciate other aspects of themselves or life. Theirs was a shallow existence. They would perform from club to club and go from one audition to the next. Their lives were on automatic pilot as they strove for and waited for that big break, that day somewhere in the future when they would finally be happy.

Funny Man, Sad Story

One Saturday night in 1986, I was performing at Dangerfield's comedy club in Manhattan. I had just finished my show and the emcee was making his final announcements when I noticed someone approaching the stage. No introduction was necessary. Rodney Dangerfield was at the pinnacle of his career and everyone knew who he was. Wearing his trademark white shirt and red tie, the star stepped into the spotlight to a thunderous round of applause. He bowed and waved to the standing and cheering fans who were chanting his name. It was deafening in that room.

I was in total awe at the energy this guy radiated. He told a few jokes, thanked the audience for supporting comedy, and stepped off the stage. People were begging him for his autograph. Some simply wanted to touch him and thank him. Then everyone started chanting that he was number one. I said to myself, "So that's what it's like to be a star."

Later that night when the crowd was gone and the staff was cleaning up, I sat at the bar with Rodney. I asked him how it felt to be at the top. He downed a double scotch and said, "It sucks." I laughed and waited for a punch line. Then it became obvious that he was serious. He proceeded to go on a verbal rampage about how he was cheated in life and that the entertainment business never gave him the respect he deserved, an eerie echo of the catchphrase that made him famous to begin with. "Look at me!" he said angrily. "They waited until my later years before they decided I was a star! I should have made it twenty or thirty years ago when I was young and I could have enjoyed it!"

I was dumbfounded. This was when Rodney's iconic performance in *Back to School*, which he starred in and cowrote, was currently showing in theaters. I searched for the right words and finally said, "But you're at the top of your career. You're a household name. Everyone knows who you are. Didn't you hear that crowd? They love you and know your jokes by heart. You have a blockbuster movie that's getting great reviews. Leonard Maltin gave you a nine!"

He downed another drink and said, "It should have been a ten. All those years of busting my ass and taking shit from people who have no idea what talent is! I gave up everything for this damn business, and for what?" He shook his head in disgust and looked straight into my eyes. "I don't expect you to understand, Steve." He looked down into his empty glass. "It should have happened years ago when I was younger. I really could have enjoyed myself."

This is a truly sad story. Here was someone who should have been living his dream. Instead, he was living a nightmare. He achieved far more than he set out to do, but he could not enjoy the benefits of his success. Why? Because for most of his life he waited for a future event to make him happy. Many years earlier he created a belief system that signified that he couldn't and wouldn't be happy until he achieved a certain status in life. As a result he bypassed the journey toward the goal, and he let his life pass him by. His past had taken over his present, daily reality, and he was haunted by regrets of days gone by.

People who view their lives as Rodney did quite often get caught up in a perpetual cycle of unconscious thoughts that lead them to believe that success and happiness are somewhere in the future. The unfortunate truth about people with this type of mindset is that no matter what they achieve, they will have a difficult time being happy. As long as they go through life unaware that they are identifying their success and happiness with a distant goal, nothing will satisfy them, even when that goal is achieved.

The Way Toward the Goal

Here's something to consider. Let's say your goal is to become a vice president of a big company. After many years of intense stress, worry, and an avalanche of emotional, mental, and physical overload, you finally achieve your goal, along with all the wealth and prestige that comes with it. Is this success? If you consult a dictionary, the answer would be yes. Webster's dictionary defines success as: "1. The favorable or prosperous termination of attempts or endeavors. 2. The attainment of wealth, position, honors, or the like." I think it's amazing that the words *happy* or *happiness* are not included in the definition of the word. Unfortunately, our conventional definition of success is simply achieving the goal. Not enough emphasis is placed on the value of experiencing the journey, building character, and learning life lessons along the way.

Here is a hypothetical question: What if someone were to show you a video of yourself as you climbed the ladder to great success? In this video you see yourself achieving all of your goals and obtaining wealth. However, you also witness how you subjected your body, mind, and spirit to intense negative energy along the way. Not only were you unhappy most of the time, but you were able to see how your outright refusal to allow for joy during the process affected your family, friends, and associates. Talk about a downer of a movie. I'll ask you the question again. Is this success?

If the process of fulfilling your goal is polluted with negative energy and lack of enjoyment, it can only create more unhappiness, even if the outcome is positive in the short term. The happiness that you feel in the moment of reaching "success" is a temporary state dictated by its conventional definition. After the initial euphoria wears off, you are back in the same old negative place. It's a sad, classic cycle of "what you sow is what you reap."

The truth is, it really doesn't matter how much money you have, or how famous you are, or how many goals you've achieved. It makes no difference how big your house is or what industry accolades you've racked up in your career. The entire world can view your life as the ultimate success story, but the bottom line is this: if you are not happy you are not successful! If you are not enjoying yourself on your journey toward your goal, you're ripping yourself off. Trust me, there are enough other people willing to do that for you.

The adventure toward any goal is what brings value to it. The path toward the goal is where your life unfolds and happiness is truly meaningful. When you are in the process of working to achieve something, you are experiencing who you are and what you're made of. Your character is being tested and molded. When you become aware of the importance of every step in the process, you are sending a message to yourself, as well as the entire universe, that you are not only here, but qualified and ready to overcome obstacles along the way. All of which are essential ingredients for happiness. Look at it this way: Isn't preparing a home-cooked meal better than something you heat up in the microwave? All right, it isn't the greatest analogy. But I think you get the point.

Of course you should go for your goal, whatever it may be, and I sincerely hope you achieve it. I also hope, for your sake and for the sake of everyone involved in your life, that you savor every moment and choose to enjoy the ride. Look at it this way: there is a unique bond between the goal and the adventure toward it. One of George Lucas's greatest creations, Indiana Jones, must encounter all kinds of adversity on his way to acquiring whatever crazy artifact he is charged with finding. ("Why did it have to be snakes?") Try to imagine Indiana just walking down the street and happening across the idol in the street. That wouldn't be very satisfying, would it? Without a few wisecracks and whipcracks when faced with difficulty, the character would be brooding and boring. The entire value of the movie relies on how he handles the adventure and adversity faced.

Now think back to the video of your own life. See any opportunities to push back your fedora, rub your stubble thoughtfully, and grin like a big dumb kid? I'm not suggesting you live your life like it's a movie. Goodness knows there are some awful examples out there to go by. I'm just trying to illustrate how, when you look back at the mental video of your life, the value won't be in the 30-second wrap-up where you are honored for your achievements, but in the scenes in which you're not sure the whip will hold, your grip is slipping, and nothing is below except tons and tons of *snakes*.

The goal you are pursuing is the path to build character and self-esteem, and for you to express who you are along the way. If, for example, the goal is a promotion or a home sale, when it is attained, sure, you'll experience tremendous pleasure and happiness, but the euphoria of achievement cannot be sustained for an extended period of time. This is true for the realization of any material goals you set for yourself. However, if you view your journey to your goals as a means to build your character, then the happiness you feel will come from a deeper place. In other words, it's not what you get but who you become along the way that gives your life the most meaning.

When I was inducted to the Speaker Hall of Fame I was ecstatic. Hey, c'mon, it was a blast and an honor to join the likes of Art Linkletter, Tony Robbins, Ronald Reagan, Norman Vincent Peale, Jack Canfield, and Colin Powell and to receive such a prestigious award in front of my family and thousands of my peers. However, on a deeper level I understood that the award was just a symbol and what was most important was how I had overcome my own self-doubt to get to this place. When I look back at the induction ceremony, sure, I feel a rosy glow of satisfaction, but the real personal victory, what really qualified the entire experience as worthwhile, was the trials I encountered and overcame along the way. It was the courage to completely shift gears and move on from my comedy career. It was the perseverance it took to prevail in spite of tremendous fear and uncertainty. These experiences, and the self-knowledge I attained during the process, are what really matter to me and will always be the highlight of my memory.

Whatever your goals, make them happen. If your goal is to be a top salesperson or executive of a big company, go for it. Make it happen. Just understand that the prestige of being a member of an elite group, while certainly something to be proud of, is not the end result. Your happiness is, right? What truly gives your achievement meaning is the overtime you put in, your commitment to excellence, and whether you were able to enjoy your road to success and appreciate the life lessons you learned along the way.

Achievement does not make the person. The goal is just a gift. It's how you've lived and what you've done to achieve the goal that brings value to it. It's the challenges that dare you to learn and grow that make you who you are. It's the people you meet along the way. When you choose to adhere to this creed, then you will have no problem appreciating and enjoying what you have, because you will be fully aware of how you earned it. Remember, the American dream is not entirely about crossing the finish line first and accepting your place atop the podium. There's a little part about the pursuit as well.

Our Main Purpose

We always have enough to be happy if we are enjoying what we do have—and not worrying about what we don't have.

KEN KEYES JR.

Some time ago, I was on a red-eye flight from Salt Lake City to New York. I was exhausted and looking forward to getting some sleep; however, the man sitting next to me was in the mood to talk.

"Is New York home," he asked, "or are you going there on business?" Before I answered him I noticed he was holding a venti-sized Starbucks coffee.

"I'm going home," I told him as I tried to get comfortable. I thought to myself, "I sure hope that's decaf."

I closed my eyes, hoping he would get the hint or maybe strike up a conversation elsewhere. He was not deterred.

"I'm going to New York to visit some friends," he continued. "The last time I was there it was during 9/11. I wound up staying a week longer than I wanted. What about you? Where were you during 9/11? Were you home or somewhere else?"

"Damn," I thought. "It's not decaf."

I realized I wasn't about to get any sleep, but I began to think that maybe I wasn't supposed to. Maybe there was something I needed to learn from this overcaffeinated chatterbox. I can't tell you how many opportunities, insights, and answers to prayers have come to me simply by allowing for a conversation with a stranger, and this particular one was no exception.

My flight companion continued asking questions, so our conversation carried on. Then he asked me something that took me by surprise: "Why do you want to be happy?" It was a simple question, but I had difficulty articulating an answer. It had never occurred to me that anyone would question the motive of happiness. I mean, I had been asked what makes me happy, and what I think happiness means. I had never been asked why I want to be happy. That's like asking why you don't want to be sad. Your first thought is, "Well, duh! Being happy is good. Being unhappy is not." Then you start to feel a little dumb.

After taking a few moments to reflect, I said, "I want to be happy because being happy makes me feel good, and feeling good makes me happy."

He motioned for me to continue.

"That's it," I said. "That's all I can think of."

"Wow," he said. "You must have people on the edge of their seats with that wisdom." We both laughed and I assured him I would have a more satisfying answer after I got some rest.

A few hours later, having overcome his caffeine rush, my seatmate was asleep. The plane was almost entirely dark as I sat, now wide awake, in a spotlight of illumination beneath the overhead light. I pondered his question.

"Why do I want to be happy?" I asked myself.

I took a hotel pad and pen from my briefcase and began to jot down my thoughts. After all, I owed my inquisitive friend an answer more befitting an expert on the power of happiness. What I came up with is neither poignant nor particularly profound, but rather a simple, honest response to his question.

I want to be happy because it makes me feel good. When I feel good, I know I'm connected to my higher self. When I'm connected to my higher self, my life flows, I lose any feeling of self-consciousness, and I find myself making choices that contribute to desired outcomes. When I'm in a state of happiness, problems and challenges are easier to handle. I don't feel singled out or unfairly targeted by little obstacles that inevitably come my way, but view them as a part of the natural process. I am filled with hope and appreciation for life's choices. But most importantly, when I'm happy, I know I'm living in the moment. I'm not living with regret over something that happened in the past, and I'm not worrying about something that might or might not happen in the future. When I'm happy, I'm simply enjoying whatever it is that I'm doing.

When I'm unhappy, I feel off-center. When I'm in a bad mood, there's a disconnect with my higher self and my life is out of whack. When I'm unhappy I feel victimized by my problems, as if the entire universe is against me. The negative emotions that result in my being unhappy become roadblocks to productivity. I feel helpless and hopeless.

Satisfied with my answer, I put down my pen and immediately felt something inside me click. Accompanied by what seemed to be the faint sound of a choir singing sweetly from somewhere up high, I came to the sudden realization, shared by philosophers, spiritualists, and great minds before me, that happiness is our main purpose and ultimate goal in life. Well, duh, indeed!

Aristotle wrote, "Happiness is the meaning and purpose in life, the whole aim and end of human existence."

In his book *Happier*, Dr. Tal Ben-Shahar writes, "Happiness is the highest on all the hierarchy of goals, the end toward which all other ends lead . . . wealth, fame, admiration, and all other goals are subordinate and secondary to happiness; whether our desires are material or social, they are means toward one end: happiness."

So I want you to understand that happiness is our main purpose and ultimate goal in life. It is the Big Kahuna and the highest of all goals. Although you may not be consciously aware of it, on a deeper level, you believe all other goals, personally and professionally, be they fame, wealth, power, marriage, raising a family, or pursuing a career, will make you become automatically, magically happy, but actually they are incidental to your happiness. Follow me on this.

Why do you want a new car? Because you believe it will make you happy. Why do you want a beautiful home in a nice neighborhood? Because you believe it will make you happy. Why do you want to save and invest your money? Because you believe it will make you happy.

Now let's focus on your desire for a relationship. Why do you want to get married? Because you're insane! (Just kidding, Gina!) Of course, you want to get married because you believe it will make you happy. Why do you want to get divorced? Because you know it will make you happy! (Really, really just kidding, Gina!)

Now, you might say that these things have nothing to do with making you happy. You might say they simply make you feel successful, special, or important. Or maybe you feel they give your life meaning. Perhaps they make you feel complete or fulfilled. But you need to ask yourself why you want to feel successful, special, or important. Ask yourself why you want to feel complete or fulfilled. Your answer will always be that you believe that, somehow, these qualities will make you happy.

Now, here's my point. Of course we want "things" that can improve our quality of life. I know I do. It's part of being human. Promotions can make us richer and allow us to feel successful. Nice homes can make us appreciate the comfort of a beautiful space to live in. And the intimacy of a satisfying relationship can provide a partner and companionship in a world that sometimes seems crazy. So . . . can these qualities bring you pleasure and give your life meaning?

Absolutely! But remember, things in themselves cannot bring you true lasting happiness. There's more to it than that.

What if, while you're driving the car that you thought would make you happy, you're in an accident and it never drives the same again? Or what if that beautiful home that you thought would make you happy is robbed? Your family heirlooms are stolen and other valuables are destroyed. To make matters worse, the insurance company that claimed that you are "in good hands" suddenly seems to be giving you the finger? The bottom line: happiness does not come from things in themselves. Happiness comes from who you are "being" at any given moment.

I'm here to tell you that it's not your goal but how you get there that's most important. It's the experience you have and how you deal with the roller coaster of life that will ultimately define whether you are truly happy. In fact, these are the essential ingredients to the recipe for happiness.

I understand that achieving a goal and having material things can make you feel good, or even ecstatic, but the truth is they are not ingredients for true happiness. They simply add flavor to the experience. Don't get me wrong, flavor is great, but the taste doesn't last that long and it's not nourishing to the soul.

I can sense your confusion here. "But Stevie," you ask, "isn't there some kind of logic in these feelings equating to happiness? After all, if I feel successful, comfortable, fulfilled, then I'm pretty sure I'll also be happy."

First of all, please don't call me Stevie. That name is reserved for use by my aunts only. Secondly, once again, happiness isn't exactly something you can just be. Remember the pursuit? Happiness is a trained behavior. If you don't enjoy the pursuit then there won't ever be quite enough success, satisfaction, or comfort to allow you to experience a deeper kind of true happiness.

Make Happiness Your Number One Priority

The problem we have is that we're not fully aware that happiness is our main purpose and ultimate goal in life. After years of concentrating on the next weekend, paycheck, raise, or family milestone, it's easy to lose track of why we work so hard, what our lives are ultimately all about. It took me hundreds of speeches on *the very subject of happiness* to realize what any five-year-old would probably tell you: it's about *being* happy. So it makes sense that if you are unaware that happiness is your ultimate goal, you won't understand the importance of living your life in a manner that will help you attain it. What am I getting at? I have absolutely no idea. Where was I? Just kidding, I'm still in control here. Bear with me as I elaborate.

Our culture teaches us that things outside ourselves make us happy, whether they are material or the realization of a goal. A distinction is not made between the relative happiness and relief that the attainment of our desires brings, and a deeper, truer happiness that is unaffected by life's ups and downs. Once we realize that the latter kind of happiness, a deeper, truer happiness, is our main purpose and ultimate goal in life, everything gets a whole lot easier.

When we recognize and understand that happiness is our main purpose and ultimate goal in life, then we can choose to make it the cornerstone of everything we set out to do. Instead of waiting for a distant goal or future event or material thing to make us happy, we make the conscious choice every day to enjoy ourselves during the process of whatever it is that we are doing. In other words, we make a conscious choice every day to make happiness our number one priority.

Right now, you might be thinking, "Give me a break, Steve-o. Let's get real here. I'd love to be happier than I am, but I have way too many problems and responsibilities to make happiness my number one priority. Isn't that being a little selfish? Besides, it's not that easy to just make a decision to be happy. That seems naïve."

I understand your concern. Sometimes the odds of trying to live a happy life are against us. That's why so many people abuse drugs and alcohol and indulge in other toxic habits. And then there is the genetic factor. Thanks to the science of positive psychology we now know that some of us are born with the happy gene and some of us aren't.

Researchers have found that we come into the world with a certain set point—a fixed degree or level of happiness—and guess what? We're stuck with it. Now, don't get your bowels in an uproar. Before you blame your mom or dad or both for your lack of enthusiasm and Eeyore attitude, there is hope. There is always hope. Even though your potential for happiness may be genetically impaired, happiness is a learned behavior, and you can learn to be happier than you ever imagined.

Today, any number of books and classes are available to us that help us make the shift to take actions toward a more positive, happy life. The leading spokesperson and father of positive psychology, Martin Seligman, PhD, created such a class at the University of Pennsylvania Positive Psychology Center. Another positive psychology class taught by Tal Ben-Shahar (whom I referenced earlier) is the most popular course at Harvard University. These classes identify characteristics and strategies of people with positive outlooks and explain how you can cultivate and experience happiness as your dominant life state, regardless of your genetic makeup.

I'll get to how you can make conscious decisions that work to make you happy later, but for now, let's talk about why you deserve happiness, even though you may feel like you haven't earned it.

Making happiness your number one priority every day is actually the most natural thing you can do for yourself and your biggest responsibility. Why? Because human beings are meant to be happy. In fact your natural state is that of joy and inner peace. You were born into this world in that state. We all were. And it is your responsibility to make the effort to stay connected to that state each and every day throughout your life. When you are in tune with your natural state, you are able to handle conflict and chaos more easily. When you're *not* in tune with your natural state, even the slightest obstacle or the simplest task can appear overwhelming and send you spinning out of control. In other words, when you're happy and in tune with your natural state, your life works more smoothly. When you aren't, your life can become out of sync and full of suffering.

I understand all too well how easy it is to get so caught up in the hustle and bustle of trying to make a living that we forget the joy of life. More often than not, throughout the course of a hectic day we become blinded to all the good that is around us. When our lives become burdened with responsibilities and problems, we forget that we should take time out and shift our focus to appreciate what is working rather than obsessing over what isn't. We don't give ourselves permission to take time out to laugh out loud at the absurdity and craziness that surrounds us.

It's a well-known fact that every time you laugh your body releases chemicals called endorphins. Endorphins are naturally manufactured by the body to relieve pain. Usually produced during periods of extreme stress, they block pain signals that are triggered by the nervous system. They actually put you in a happier state.

But instead of letting biology do its job, we compound our stress by getting frustrated and angry. We forget what a simple favor we're doing ourselves when we occasionally step out of the grinding daily monotony and appreciate the simple aspects of our lives.

I'll give you an example. Doing what I do, I fly well over 200,000 miles a year. To put that in perspective, the arctic tern, the bird species with the longest migration, of about 24,000 miles a year, flies from pole to pole, stopping to mate only once every one to three years. I manage to schedule a few more mating sessions than that, but I digress.

Sometimes I'm in seven cities in ten days. Sometimes I have a half-day seminar to give and my butt is dragging on the floor. You know the feeling. One thing that lifts my spirits is when I make the shift and turn the funny side of me loose in a public setting. When others laugh along with me, I get an extra boost of energy, everyone has a good time, and that butt-dragging-on-the-floor feeling goes away. I feel lighter and more in touch with the world around me. Of course, there are other times when I pull things in a more private setting. The person I'm talking to doesn't get that I'm joking and doesn't know how to respond. That really cracks me up, too.

Here's a little example. Since I travel a lot, I also spend a great part of my life in hotels, and I'm always having fun with the hotel staff. One afternoon I was working in my room when the maid service knocked on the door. "Mr. Rizzo, can I turn down your bed?" she asked me. I looked at her and said, "Why, is it too loud?" You should have seen the puzzled look on her face as she walked away, mumbling something about the crazy man in room 325. She didn't get it, but I did, and that was all right.

When I returned later that night the bedsheets were indeed turned down. Don't get me wrong, I think turndown is a wonderful service, but for the life of me I can't understand why a piece of chocolate is left on your pillow. I started thinking, "Hmmm. Don't hotel people know what we all know? Chocolate does not help you sleep!" In fact, the caffeine gives it the complete opposite effect. Laughing at the absurdity of this ritual, I decided to have a little fun and called the front desk the next morning.

Bright and cheerful, the concierge answered, "How can I be of service this morning, Mr. Rizzo?"

"Oh," I replied, "I'm just calling to thank you for the chocolate that was on my pillow last night. It really helped me sleep."

"You are most welcome. I'm glad you slept well, Mr. Rizzo. Is there anything else we can do for you?"

"Yes, as a matter of fact there is," I continued. "I was wondering if maybe tonight you could put a vial of crack and a pot of coffee on my pillow. I think that would help me sleep."

Three seconds went by before I was answered.

"Oh, I don't think we can do that!"

That's right, someone else who just didn't get it. But just because they don't get it doesn't mean I can't have fun. I'm not saying that you should try to make other people uncomfortable. However, I believe that challenging the serious nature of others is a great way to remind yourself and them that there is a time and place for being serious, and that everyone can use a laugh now and then.

When I made the decision to make happiness my number one priority every day, I became aware of a whole new world of possibilities. Healthier choices instantly presented themselves. I learned how to make myself feel better when times were tough simply by shifting my thoughts and focusing on something that would lift my spirits. I began to create habits and develop mindsets that enabled me to live more in the moment and to enjoy myself during the process.

Let me make this perfectly clear. I'm in no way suggesting that if you make happiness your number one priority and use the tools in this book, that you will live happily ever after, 24/7/365. Give me a break. This is a personal development book, not a prescription for antidepressants or a Disney movie. To expect to be happy all the time is to set yourself up for disappointment and failure. Furthermore, if you were happy all of the time, its meaning would be completely lost because you would have nothing to compare it with.

Experiencing true happiness invariably involves emotional discomfort and difficult experiences along the way. In fact, it depends on them. Our challenges build our character and self-esteem. How we approach and respond to these challenges is what determines the quality of our happiness. A happy person can experience highs and lows throughout their life while maintaining a positive outlook on their life as a whole.

The goal isn't to be in a perpetual state of Pollyannaish happiness. Rather, the goal is to realize that if you stay conscious of your ability to shift into a feel-good state of mind and allow it to occur, happiness will come around more often than not.

Understand that you don't have to wait for something good to happen to feel good. You can view your challenges from a vantage point. You can teach yourself to appreciate the benefits of temporarily stepping away from your feelings of being overwhelmed by a difficult situation and shift your attention to that which empowers you and makes you feel good. That's what you want, isn't it? To feel good more often? Well, then, why wait for a problem to be solved or a challenge to go away before you allow yourself to feel good? Why not learn and exercise positive alternatives that will enable you to feel confident during the process of solving the problem? Why wait for some future goal to be fulfilled to be happy? Why aren't you answering me?

If you really think about it, it defies all logic. I mean, what good is achieving a goal or even setting a goal for yourself if you don't enjoy the process of fulfilling it? When you make feeling happy of paramount importance, you will seek out that which truly makes you feel happy. Taking action based on that imperative will have the result of making you feel good, no matter what your circumstances or the outcome of the problem you are facing. Remember, it's valuing the process, the journey toward your goal, the lessons learned that ultimately promotes an inner state of true happiness.

Your Overall Happiness

Let's face it. There will always be challenges and unexpected problems to deal with. Even the very fortunate among us experience setbacks and suffering of some kind at different stages in their lives. Challenges and stress are a part of life. As Frank Sinatra crooned, "That's life. That's what all the people say. You're ridin' high in April, shot down in May." He also sang, "Doobie, doobie, doo," but the relevance of that lyric totally escapes me.

My point is that you can experience unease, sadness, and pain at times and still be happy overall. Your overall happiness is determined by what you choose to focus on the most in the world from day to day. That's the key.

For example, a sunny blue sky can have scattered clouds passing by. To some, overall it's still a sunny blue sky. To others, it's a sky marred by clouds. You need to ask yourself what you focus on most in your world. Do you focus on the sunny blue sky or do you put your attention on the clouds? I'm not asking you to think literally, as if you were a meteorologist (unless you are one, of course), but as an individual with an overall worldview. Your honest answer will be in direct relation to the degree of your overall happiness. If you fit into the category of someone who sees the clouds, simply by shifting your focus to the bright blue sky, your degree of happiness is immediately elevated. That concept applies to everything in your life and is otherwise known as "seeing the glass half full." That's what we'll focus on from here.

Being the astute observer that I am, I can pretty much tell a person's degree of overall happiness on any given day just by asking a very simple question: "How are you doing today?" Their answers will vary greatly from a high degree of happiness to a very low degree of happiness.

"My life is great."

"Couldn't be better."

"Okay, I guess."

"I'll get by."

"It could be worse."

"Not so good."

"Terrible."

And my two personal favorites:

"Don't ask."

"You don't want to know!"

The responses we give can vary from day to day, depending on our circumstances and, more important, how we view them. But my goal is to bring you to a place where you will always come to a positive answer.

I saw a billboard recently that made me smile: "Don't wait for the storms of your life to pass. Learn to dance in the rain." Read that again. That statement is a touchstone for living a happier life. "Dancing in the rain" is an attitude that truly happy and successful people live by, and few dancers come by it naturally. Can you learn to dance in the rain when the storms of misfortune are pouring down on you? I believe the answer is yes. How do you acquire this attitude? By making happiness a habit. By making an effort and employing my Attitude Adjustment Strategies, you will learn to shift your focus to the sunny blue sky and the result will be a higher degree of overall happiness in your life.

So for your sake, get you shift together!

Regardless of your current overall degree of happiness, I want you to ask yourself, "Do I want to be happier than I am?" I can only assume yes, otherwise why would you be reading this? Now I'll ask another question: Are you willing to make the effort required to become happier than you are?

Before you answer, let me tell you there are no coincidences in life. Everything happens for a reason. This book is in your hands for a reason. You were drawn to it, curious about the subject and its strategies, because on some level you want to better your life. Even if your life right now is pretty great and you have a high degree of overall happiness, still, you were drawn to this book because there is some benefit to you that can be derived from it.

Okay, you can answer the question now. Forgot it already? Here's a refresher: "Am I willing to make the effort required to become happier than I am? Do I want to be happy?" Here's a hint: Yes, you do.

The Last of the Human Freedoms

We are all aware that there are people on this planet who live in horrific conditions and experience oppression of all kinds. To suggest to any such person that they should make happiness their number one priority might seem insensitive or ludicrous. Yet the truth is, even amid the most devastating of circumstances, people can make courageous choices that will allow them some degree of relief from their suffering. Let me offer up the real-life example of Viktor Frankl.

In his book *Man's Search for Meaning*, Frankl shares what he learned from his experiences as a prisoner in Auschwitz during World War II: "Everything can be taken from a man but one thing:

the last of the human freedoms—to choose one's attitude in any set of circumstances, to choose one's own way."

Read that again, and consider his situation as you do—physical and mental torture and a life seemingly with no choices. Surrounded by total despair and devastation, Frankl chose to embrace an attitude that enabled him to at the very least feel better, and at times to experience some degree of happiness that should be unimaginable considering his personal circumstances. The actions he took to help a friend to develop his sense of humor amid their shared tragedy provided both of them relief from their daily reality. Here's what they did: Frankl and his friend promised to imagine and tell each other every day some amusing incident that would happen after they were liberated. This simple act of storytelling developed into a sort of improvised cabaret, joined by other prisoners from time to time. They sang, shared poems, told jokes, and developed a keen appreciation for the power of satire. Many prisoners attended, despite their fatigue and the fact that they thereby missed their daily food rations. Their participation was effective in helping them to forget, if briefly, their dire situation.

To my mind, this shows that sometimes nourishment of the soul is more important than nourishment of the body. Humor was used as a weapon in the fight for soul preservation. It is well documented that humor, more than anything else within the human ambit of understanding, can help an individual to rise above any situation.

Even if only for a few moments at a time, Viktor Frankl did whatever he could to focus on things that would help lift his spirits. This simple act gave him an infallible attitude, the courage to dare to be at least happier than his circumstances dictated, and in the end it was responsible for his survival.

It is my belief that we all intuitively know what Frankl understood and acted upon: that happiness is our right to choose and even our destiny. It is a calling and a yearning for a higher part of ourselves, challenging us to experience a sacred "time out" for peace and joy, even under the most severe circumstances. Even if only for a few moments at a time. Sometimes, my friend, a few moments of that happiness is all you need to keep you from giving up.

Make It a Habit

> Happiness is an attitude. We either make ourselves miserable, or happy and strong. The amount of work is the same.
>
> **FRANCESCA REIGLER**

Allow me to let you in on a little secret. (No, it's not Victoria's Secret. Victoria really doesn't have a secret. Have you ever seen the merchandise in that store? It's obvious the secret is pretty much revealed.) Are you ready? Here it is: Happiness is a choice—*that's it*. It's a little secret, right? But a great one. Happiness is a choice. That's all you need to know. You are now enlightened. You can close this book and go about your business. Congratulations on your newfound self-awareness. Hey, I'm kidding, all right? But it is true. Happiness is a choice. As I stated earlier, making happiness a choice is what it's all about.

So . . . I know right about now you're thinking, "If happiness is a choice, then why are so many people feeling crappy instead of happy? Why are so many people going through life feeling unfulfilled?" The answer is that most people either don't believe that happiness is a choice or can't understand its meaning. As Abraham Lincoln once said, "People are about as happy as they make up their minds to be." And this coming from a man who had the weight of an entire fractured country on his shoulders.

Okay, so what do I mean by "happiness is a choice"? I think people can reject this notion out of hand because it is so simply phrased. "Oh, you mean all I have to do is make a choice and, presto, I'm happy? Give me a break, Sparky!"

No, that's not what I mean. And don't call me Sparky!

Happiness isn't one choice, like deciding which presidential candidate will make you less miserable or picking between the chicken and the prime rib. Instead, happiness is a long, continuous choice. If that notion seems too daunting, try thinking of it as a lifetime of small, moment-to-moment choices.

On any given day there are a number of reasons/excuses that I can use to justify being unhappy. It can be work-related, family issues (if you knew my family you would definitely understand), time constraints, or someone else's bad mood. The key, however, is that I know I'm responsible for my own state of mind. I am totally aware of what happens to me when I begin to lose the thread of that control. Allowing these outside forces or circumstances to determine my happiness can quickly send me into a downward spiral. The same goes for you. Whatever it is that has the potential to keep you from enjoying the day and the success you desire, understand that it's not the situation itself that is causing you to be unhappy or to feel unsuccessful. It's really the thoughts you have about the situation. It's what you choose to focus on that fuels your emotions and defines your reality, as you will see in the following story.

One day I was walking along a pier in San Diego when I noticed a young woman dancing and singing softly to herself. Occasionally she would stop and take a sip of her coffee. As I walked by she waved and smiled, and this wasn't just a run-of-the-mill, everyday smile. It was a radiant smile and it was accompanied by an exuberant glow. I mean, I actually felt uplifted by that smile.

"Someone is happy today," I said.

Her reply was, "What's not to be happy about? The sun is shining.

It's a beautiful morning. I have a delicious cup of coffee and last night I was at a concert and the lead singer was singing directly to me. Life is wonderful."

I have to admit that I was impressed and intrigued (and wondering if I could have some of whatever was in her coffee). "Are you always like this?" I asked.

"Yes," she said. "For the most part I am. It doesn't take that much to make me happy."

Now she really had my attention. "Don't you ever have problems or get in a bad mood?" I asked.

This made her laugh. "Of course I do," she said. "I just know that bad moods are a choice and problems are relative. I try to look at a problem as something I need to learn. If I do learn from it, then it isn't a problem. It's a gift." She took a sip of her evidently delicious coffee and then continued, "In fact, just this morning I couldn't start my car. Sure, I was getting frustrated. I mean, I just bought it last week! It's brand-new and I was late for work. Anyway, the good news in all this is that my neighbor noticed I was having difficulty and she offered to give me a ride to work." She beamed that radiant smile of hers again. "You know," she continued, "in the two years I lived next door to her, I knew nothing about her. I mean, she's my neighbor, for crying out loud! We had a wonderful conversation and we're going out for dinner tonight. So, yes, my new car wouldn't start, but I believe because of that I have a new friend. I choose to focus on that. That's the gift within the problem."

If we could all see our problems and mishaps from the viewpoint of the young woman with the radiant smile, life would be much easier, wouldn't it? She is living proof that it all comes down to choices. Rather than dwell on negativity, you can choose to focus on what is working in your life, to be grateful for what you have, and to use your time and energy finding solutions to your problems. If you do, you will be nourishing your soul and experiencing a happier, healthier reality for yourself. Either way, the outcome is based on choices. Choose to be happy now, no matter what is happening around you. If you wait for something else to change first, you don't stand a chance at happiness. How's that for delivering the truth?

The same incident can be experienced and interpreted in different ways by different people. There are those who view little mishaps as major catastrophes, while others find the humor in them. Some people would have their day ruined if their car didn't start. These kinds of people have a tendency to intensify their problems by continuously rehashing their woe-is-me story. This is an attitude that stifles soul growth. That's not to say that you're wrong to get upset when your car doesn't start and you're late for work. That's natural, of course. But you're doing yourself a grave disservice if you allow the bad mood to continue. If you're not vigilant, one bad mood can snowball out of control and ruin what could otherwise be an enjoyable and productive day.

Ralph Waldo Emerson had it right when he said, "To different minds, the same world is a hell and a heaven." The girl with the radiant smile was determined to always choose her own focus. When her car wouldn't start, she chose to focus on making a new friend. I don't know this young woman personally, but I'm going to make an educated guess that she views most of the events in her life from that same healthy perspective. What a great way to live! Don't give your peace and happiness away. Think of the repercussions if you do. You could be relying on your car's starter for your happiness for the rest of your life.

Here's an idea. Why not make happiness a habit in your life? That's exactly what I did, and I firmly believe that if I could do it, anyone can. Here's how. From here until the end of the book you will learn how to apply and use the Attitude Adjustment Strategies into every aspect of your life. No, really!

Rise and Shine

Let's get started. Right now I want you to begin the process of internalizing that happiness is your main purpose and ultimate goal in life. I want you to make a conscious choice *every day* to enjoy yourself during the process of whatever it is you are trying to achieve. This goes for everything. You can apply this shift of attitude to even the most mundane or unpleasant tasks. Don't reserve it for just your personal and professional goals, but for all the daily choices you make. Whether you are giving the dog a bath, spending time with your children, cleaning the house, starting an exercise program, watching TV, or performing a task at work, make enjoying yourself your number one priority. (If you happen to be an undertaker or postal worker, just do your best.)

Here's another question: What do you think of when someone says, "Rise and shine"? (Besides wanting to kill them, of course, because invariably you're sound asleep and they've woken you.) "Rise and shine" is a well-worn idiom, but it really holds power as long as you take it literally. I mean, does "Wake and be grateful" have the same punch to it? Ultimately this cheery, time-tested phrase simply suggests that the beginning of your day should be the most positive part of your day. You really should "shine."

I can just see you people reading this now. "Morning folks" are nodding. Non-morning people are sharpening their knives. Subscribing to the "Rise and shine" way of life doesn't mean that you have to arise before 5 a.m. or anytime in particular, just that whenever you do arise, give yourself the best few minutes of consciousness that you can before everyone else jumps in. You can teach yourself to do this, and it will make a huge difference in how you face life each day.

First you need a regular routine to get in the happiness habit. Begin by creating a daily foundation for a mindset that's open to happiness. It starts as soon as you wake up in the morning—or, if you're a student, in the afternoon. Whenever you first rise, it's important to set your mental stage and your emotional gauge to feel good. Why first thing when you wake up? Because the moment when you first open your eyes is when you leave your dreams and emerge into consciousness. Your creativity and ability to dictate the tone of the day is at its most powerful. It is the best opportunity you'll have to steer your thoughts and emotions in the direction that will enable you to create a day that you can enjoy, regardless of what you'll be doing. And when you first wake, your mind is most susceptible to messages of any kind. After all, you've just spent the night doing whatever your subconscious mind tells you, so take advantage of this window when you're completely open to suggestion. Set a precedent for how the rest of the day is going to unfold. Choose to seize the day or let the day seize you. Or you can seize your alarm clock, throw it against the wall, and come back to this part later.

So . . . as soon as you open your eyes, know that you are the creator of your day. Resist the urge to go over your to-do list; instead, think of who you have to be in order to handle the challenges of the coming day.

Your first decision as creator is to focus on something that pleases you. Don't think of the traffic jam you're going to be stuck in or the bad day you had yesterday. Your only goal here is simply to raise your energy level and to feel good, whatever that means to you. Focus on the person lying next to you or the comfort of the room, or photographs of happy times with family and friends. Relive one of these wonderful memories or allow your attention to settle on the sound of the birds outside your window, or the dog lying at the foot of the bed. It really doesn't matter what it is, just as long as you hold your attention on it long enough to notice how wonderful it feels to have these things in your life. Once again, your only goal here is to make yourself feel good right at the beginning of the day.

Once you settle into the feeling of well-being that this exercise provides, take it a step further. Now focus on someone or something that you are totally grateful for. Again, it doesn't matter what it is. It can be a person, a pet, the achievement of a past goal, your garden, a hobby, the neighborhood you live in, something somebody did for you, or something you did for someone else. Dial into your gratitude for whatever you're thinking about, and feel it with your heart and soul.

This is important. If you're not really feeling it or if you're forcing it because you're hungry and want your Pop-Tart already, the exercise will be less effective. (Or you could just be grateful for that Pop-Tart you're about to consume!) Consider the act of being truly grateful as if it were vitamins for your day. Commit to something. Why? Because gratitude is the most powerful connection you have to your higher self, God, the divine, or whatever you want to call it. The point is that you always want to keep your connection to this higher part of yourself. The stronger that connection, the better you feel. The better you feel, the more creative and productive you are. The more creative and productive you are, the better you feel. When you fully appreciate what you have in the moment, good things come into your life. Why? Because the gratitude bone is connected to the happiness bone, and it's this fun little cycle that eventually acts as a magnet to attract the things you desire most, whatever they might be, into your life.

Here's my challenge to you: try this exercise for three days in a row. Before you get out of bed, consciously focus on how grateful you are for something that you have. Make it part of your waking process and you will engage your subconscious, that great misunderstood mind that basically runs your life. I guarantee that within three short days you will begin to feel better about your life. It isn't magic; it's taking the steps to create a healthier mindset day by day and building a pathway to making happiness a habit and creating the life you want.

This is not Pollyannaish mumbo-jumbo. Scientists and mental health experts teach us that our lives move in the direction of our most dominant thoughts. So if you are consistent about creating thoughts about abundance and success, and are consciously grateful for the things you already have, you'll not only find yourself moving toward the things you want, but you will also draw them toward you. This mindset has to start as soon as you start the day, so don't let me catch you being grateful at dinnertime!

Some of you may be thinking that there is too much pain and worry in your life to be grateful for anything. But no matter how low you may feel or how bad things are, there is always something to be grateful for, and it is your job to dig deep, find it, and praise it. A perfect example of someone in dire straits who managed to feel grateful every day is Christopher Reeve, the actor who played Superman in the 1978 film and its sequels.

Christopher Reeve, thrown from a horse in an equestrian competition in 1995, was paralyzed from the neck down. Even though the odds were against his survival, he was determined to live and enjoy his life, thus becoming a true superhero.

In those early days following his accident, Chris was so overwhelmed by his dismal condition that he thought about taking his own life. Needless to say, he could find nothing to be grateful for. But his wife, Dana, knelt by his bed and said the words that soothed his soul: "You're still you and I love you." And when he saw the faces of his three children as they entered his hospital room, he knew in an instant that they wanted him to live and be there for them in the now. It was at that moment that Christopher Reeve found his purpose and something to be grateful for, and he held on to it. This sense of appreciation that he could still be there for his children ignited a spark in him that caused him to begin thinking of options for a way to live his life fully despite his debilitating physical condition.

Many of us heard Chris proclaim to the world that one day he would walk again. This was a bold and hopeful statement, and although he failed to reach that goal, what was more important is what he did with his life with the time he had. The man in the wheelchair accomplished more in the last nine years of his life than most people do in a lifetime. He was chairman of the board of the Christopher Reeve Paralysis Foundation, vice chairman of the National Organization on Disability, and an active lobbyist for stem cell research. He was the author of two bestselling books, *Still Me* and *Nothing Is Impossible*. He directed, produced, and acted in movies. And in his spare time he spoke throughout the country and parts of the world on how to embrace adversity.

Undoubtedly one of the reasons Christopher Reeve was able to live such a fulfilling life was because he was able to hold on to what he was grateful for. Gratitude for his family was his foundation, and he built his life on and around it. His legacy is one of hope, showing us all how to persevere through the most challenging times and how to be grateful for what we have, even when it may not seem like much.

In 2001, Chris said, "I'm not living the life I thought I would lead, but it does have meaning and purpose. There is love, there is joy, and there is laughter." Read that again and then tell me you can't find something for which to be grateful.

Finding something to be grateful for can take work, but you'll discover it is well worth the effort. Sometimes you have to push yourself, especially when negative emotions about the coming day are getting the best of you. (Does dreading a meeting with the boss ring a bell? If it doesn't, then *you* are probably the boss, so quit giving everybody a hard time!) I have found that when I'm having trouble being grateful, the best thing for me to do is to become absolutely still, dig deep, and become aware of the fear, anger, guilt, or whatever emotion has its claws in me.

Becoming aware of your negative emotions does not mean that you hold on to them and analyze them with intensity. In fact, it's the complete opposite. It simply means that you observe them without judgment as they pass through your mind. No need to give them any attention. You already know they're bad for you, so why attract their attention to you? This is really a great experience, because as you allow the negativity to pass, you actually feel your energy level elevate. Sometimes I have a little fun with this and physically wave to the negative feelings as they leave my body. "Bye-bye," I say. "Have a nice day. I know I will. Don't let the door hit you in the ass on your way out."

Later on, I will explain in more detail about the importance of becoming aware of negative emotions. For now, just know that when you become aware of any negative emotion, you actually help break the self-identification you have with it and you are able to come back to the present moment. This puts you once again in touch with the power you have to seize the day and realize, once again, that it's all up to you. Hey, that alone is something to be grateful for. Build on that.

I cannot stress this enough, but I'll try. There is always, always, always, and always something to be grateful for. Always! When you discover it, feel it with everything you've got and then build from there. This is especially important at the beginning of your day. Feeling grateful and appreciative is the fastest way to turn your life around.

ATTITUDE ADJUSTMENT STRATEGY:
Practice shifting into a state of feeling good.

Whenever you first rise, always set your mental stage and emotional gauge to feel good. Know that the creation of your day is about to begin and that you alone are its director. Your first decision is to focus on the things that please you and the things that you are grateful for. Your goal is to simply raise your energy level to feel good.

"I'm Going to Enjoy This Day!"

Now that you've made the choice to start your day by creating a state of feeling good and an attitude of gratitude, the next step is to declare to yourself and the entire universe that you are going to enjoy the day. Once again, this is not some kind of Pollyannaish mumbo-jumbo. The words of encouragement, hope, and joy that you speak out loud are like seeds that will always bear fruit that's nourishing to the soul. Words that signify lack, chaos, and hopelessness will always bear fruit that will no doubt give your soul, at the very least, indigestion. So instead of complaining about the way things are going to be, start declaring the way you want things to be.

As soon as you've expressed internal gratitude for something, get out of bed and plant your feet on the ground and say (preferably out loud, depending on who is still sleeping), "I'm going to enjoy this day!"

Say it with conviction.

"I'm going to enjoy this day!"

Say it as you are taking a shower and as you are getting dressed. Announce it to your toaster.

"Good morning, toaster! Did you know that I'm going to enjoy this day?"

If it answers back, seek help immediately.

Say it as you're eating breakfast. But please make sure you have chewed your food. There is no need to be disgusting.

"I'm going to enjoy this day!"

Every now and then, throw in "Happiness is my number one priority today!" And I also suggest an occasional affirmation. My favorite: "Whatever this day brings, there's that in me that is strong enough to meet it and to be blessed by it." And continue to put your attention on that which you are grateful for. If you get your words and attitude going in the right direction you will notice a shift in the way your day and your life are going.

As you are reciting your affirmations and proclaiming your joy to the world, there's something you can add—imagine yourself enjoying and even laughing during the activities of the coming day. The key to making visualization effective is to have fun with it and to do it with passion. See and feel the excitement of your day as it unfolds. Include every detail. See yourself succeeding in all of your business endeavors.

For example, if you have an important meeting to attend or a proposal to make, envision yourself feeling confident and energized. Imagine yourself having fun with coworkers, associates, or whoever is involved. Visualize yourself being congratulated for a job well done.

If you are in sales, see yourself with total confidence as you're closing a deal.

If you're a nurse, see yourself laughing with your patients and their families and as you interact with your coworkers.

If you are a teacher, envision yourself connecting with your students.

If traffic is always a problem on your commute (a favorite of mine, if you haven't guessed by now), plan ahead and imagine yourself being calm. Know that you can't control the traffic, but you can control your emotions. For an extra boost, always have your favorite music, audiobooks, or comedians available for your listening pleasure. Visualize yourself singing or laughing behind the wheel as everyone else gets angry, bored, and frustrated.

Visualizing how you want your day to go instills faith, along with increased desire and intention that will power you through your day. And then, when that something wonderful happens, or you find yourself actually enjoying the day and the people you come into contact with, the whole cycle will be reinforced, and negative emotions will be easier to fend off.

The point is that you want to start your day off with high energy and a positive attitude. Too many people start their day in a bad or low mood at best. And what makes it worse is that they have no idea why. That is to say, people may not be conscious that they are focusing on what is broken and not what can be created from their day. As soon as they open their eyes, they start to go over their problems, thinking about, even visualizing, the chaos from the day before and the grueling one that lies ahead. If only they understood that they can choose alternatives that will help them enjoy the day. Because they may be so caught up in the insanity of whatever their current situation may be, there is no room in their head for thoughts that are healthier and more productive. If only they would switch their focus to things that make them feel good, they could at least get some relief from the bombardment of negativity that assaults their morning ritual.

But now that *you* have established a positive morning routine, don't think you're off the hook and that later in the day you can go back to your old way of thinking. It's important that you keep an attitude of gratitude throughout the day.

For example, let's say you're driving through or flying over some beautiful landscape that touches you in some way. Don't let the feeling pass. Hold on to it. Savor it. Let yourself feel the wonder of it and allow your heart to soar. If you witness an act of kindness that puts a smile on your face, hold on to that as a reminder of how won-derful people can be and do something at least as kind in the next 24 hours. If someone says, "Have a nice day," don't just let it slide. Ac-knowledge the person and say, "Hey, don't tell me what to do! This is going to be a crappy day and your telling me to have a nice one just made it worse." I'm obviously having some fun here. A better response might be, "You know what? I will have a nice day. Thank you. You do the same."

The greatest benefit of genuinely enjoying the day is that you generate a massive amount of positive energy. It's manifested in pas-sion and enthusiasm, and both are very contagious. Put another way, enjoyment is the spark that ignites passion and enthusiasm. Read that again and remember it. C'mon, I said read it again!

I'm not claiming that by making a commitment to enjoy the day you won't be confronted by challenges. Of course you will! There will always be obstacles of some kind to overcome. True, there will be times when chaos and negative forces surround you, but you don't have to let them inside. It may not be easy at first, but as you condition yourself to prepare for the day ahead with gratitude, joyful statements, and positive visualization, you will notice that stressful outside forces don't bother you as much. Ultimately what you are doing is creating the ability to bounce back, and that's an all-important life skill.

It comes down to this: the unexpected is waiting for you. Countless outside factors can make or ruin your day, many of which are not in your direct control. So it makes sense to seize control of what you can. No matter whether you're in an up or down period, remind yourself that true happiness (and inner peace) is your num-ber one priority. And focusing on what makes you grateful puts you on the path to happiness and the ability to enjoy the day. And that is exactly why you have to make the shift to start your day in a good mood and maintain your feelings of appreciation throughout. Even one situation a day in which you are able to invoke your grateful feelings and choose to be happy in the moment can have a tremendous impact on your life. I don't mean to suggest that you become the Dalai Lama, but if you do, please smile and bless the rest of us.

One last point (I promise) is the necessity to take action with passion and enthusiasm, instead of just going through the motions.

When times are tough, it is passion and enthusiasm that push you to go that extra mile. Passion and enthusiasm propel you into a zone where you feel confident, courageous, and victorious. Failure is not an option and every mistake is viewed as a do-over. When something doesn't turn out the way you planned, you don't even consider defeat. You're in such a high state of mind that you'll find yourself saying, "Okay, that didn't work. What do I have to do to turn this around? Who can I go to for help?" and "I know I can do this!"

I'm repeating myself, I know, but I really want you to get this. (Plus, it's my book and I'll do what I want!) Enjoyment is the spark that ignites passion and enthusiasm. Remember that always.

ATTITUDE ADJUSTMENT STRATEGY:
Practice shifting into a state of enjoyment.

After you have shifted into a state of feeling good, get out of bed, plant your feet on the ground, and declare to the entire universe, "I'm going to enjoy this day!" and "I choose to be happy now!" Say it as you are taking a shower and getting dressed. Occasionally recite your favorite affirmation. Visualize yourself enjoying, laughing, and succeeding during activities of the coming day.

The Power of Laughter

One of my lifetime goals is to be at peace with my negative and neurotic tendencies. I no longer try to fight them or pretend they're not there. I've come to realize that they are a part of who I am and they will probably be with me forever. (Oh gee, life is a party, isn't it?) Accepting this previously unwanted part of who I am is a great relief. It's made a huge difference in how I react when they pop up and try to invade and prevail in my world. Now I simply laugh at them with great amusement. When I allow myself the freedom to crack a joke and laugh in the middle of a negative or stressful episode, these "undesirable" parts of myself actually begin to lose power. It's as if I'm saying to them, "I know you're there and I know what you're trying to do. You've had your few moments of glory. Now get lost! I have a life to enjoy!"

There is nothing like laughter that can instantly shift your mind into a good mood and help you to bounce back to enjoy the day. Not even sex has the same power—and this is coming from someone of the male gender. What I mean is that to most men sex is like pizza. When it's hot, it's great. When it's cold . . . it's still great. The point is that laughter is the instant mind shift. Got it!

Let me give you a personal example of how to take control of your emotions through humor. Years ago, in the middle of my comedy career, I was in New York City driving a rental car that kept breaking down. It was 98 degrees, the air-conditioning didn't work, and sweat was pouring from my body. To make matters worse, I was in the world's biggest traffic jam and I was already 45 minutes late for a very important audition. I started to feel an avalanche of negative emotions building up. I said to myself out loud, "What else could possibly go wrong?" I soon realized that that was the wrong question to ask. Whenever you ask a question like that the universe has its own way of answering you.

I drove up to the tollbooth with beads of sweat running down my face. I tried really hard to control my emotions. I reached into my pocket to pay the toll and immediately realized that I had left my money at home. I sat there in total amazement at the series of events that were keeping me from my destination. I started to take it personally. I actually believed something out there was gunning for me and was quickly gaining. For a moment I was in a daze. I was unaware of the cars beeping and people cursing at me. The guy in the tollbooth finally asked, "Can I help you?" I don't know what possessed me, but I said, "Yeah, I'll have a couple of burgers, two fries, a Coke, and get something for yourself there, Sparky!"

Apparently he was new to this country and didn't understand my brand of humor. "I'm sorry," he said, "but we do not have food here!"

"Well," I replied, "then you better get some, because you're holding up traffic!" As soon as I answered him, I noticed he had started to laugh. And much to my surprise, so did I. The long line of drivers behind me, however, did not join in the fun. The horns and cursing continued.

"Come on, we got to get moving!"

"What the hell is the problem up there?"

Then, to my surprise, my newfound friend stuck his head out from the tollbooth, motioned to the line of cars, and shouted, "I am very sorry, but we ran out of food. Please try the next booth!"

By then we were both hysterical over the absurdity of the situation. We were high-fiving each other and the coolest thing is that he let me go without paying. He said, "This toll is on me. Thank you! I am new to this country and this is only my second day on the job. Believe me when I say, I really needed to laugh today!" I looked at him and said, "Believe me, so did I!" We shook hands and wished each other a great day. I drove away from that tollbooth in a totally different mood, able to plant positive thoughts in my head and think of constructive ways to deal with the important audition ahead.

Guess what? I had a great audition! It's a good thing I did, because it led to the most important break in my career: the Showtime cable special, which paved the way to many other opportunities. I often ask myself, what would have happened if I had gone to the audition in the mood that I was in before the tollbooth incident? I wouldn't have had a chance. No way, not in the mood I was in. In fact, I had almost turned the car around to go home. I had tried everything to control the situation. After all, at that time in my life I thought I was an expert on positive psychology. Boy, was I ever wrong! I found out that day that positive thinking and reciting positive affirmations doesn't always work as fast as you want. There are times when you are in such an overwhelming negative emotional state that there's no way your brain is going to buy the fact that everything is okay, no matter what you tell it.

I mean, picture this. There I was, sitting behind the wheel of a stalling car without air-conditioning, sweating in a 98-degree heat wave, stuck in the world's biggest traffic jam, late for my audition, and reciting affirmations out loud over and over. "Everything is going as planned." "I am in control of this situation." "I am the radiating center of love and peace." (Yeah, right!)

Just then someone honked their horn and I motioned to him with my fist and shouted, "Pick a number, pal!" (Smart, huh?) Not only was I frustrated and angry, I also felt totally inadequate because I couldn't shift into a positive state of mind and get control of my emotions.

When I started to laugh, however, there was an instant change in my mood. I was able to calm down and actually visualize a positive outcome to my audition. Do you know why? Okay, I'll tell you. When you start laughing at a stressful or highly emotional situation your brain is no longer registering negative thoughts that serve to intensify your already out-of-control emotions. In fact, your brain is now somewhere else, laughing at something ridiculous that you just did. So even when your brain goes back to the situation at hand, you won't feel as overpowered by it as you did before, because your laughter has put a stop to the snowball effect. You have calmed down your nervous system to the point where you can actually think rationally and shift your thoughts to a more positive outcome.

You never know when opportunity is going to knock, my friend. When it does, you have to be prepared. I can't tell you how many opportunities I've blown in my life because I couldn't control my emotions. I can't tell you how many bridges I burned because I made decisions when I was in an unhealthy state of mind. It doesn't matter what you call it. You can call it karma, the law of cause and effect, or cosmic payback. It doesn't matter. The fact is that the choices you make will determine the actions you take. Sometimes, making the shift to laugh and taking a step back to reassess things from a more positive perspective seems to be the only remedy to the random craziness of life. My choice was shouting at the steering wheel, or finding humor in a stressful moment. I chose laughter. Because, really, what did my steering wheel ever do to me?

ATTITUDE ADJUSTMENT STRATEGY:
Take time out every day to find the laughter within you and all around you.

It's there. Trust me. You may have to look hard to find it, or even create it out of thin air. The easiest way to do this is to make fun of your own frustration. Take a moment to get outside of yourself and watch what happens. That's the real shift.

And I Say to Myself, "What a Wonderful World!"

Without a doubt, giving of ourselves is the one activity that makes us realize that we're all connected and that it's this connection that plays a big part in making the world a wonderful place to be. I can honestly say that I'm the happiest when I've done something nice for someone. Don't just take my word for it. Try it and see for yourself. The next time an opportunity arises, take the initiative and perform an act of kindness for someone (even a stranger) and notice how you feel.

Here's an example: the next time you're walking through town and notice a parking summons on someone's windshield, go over to the car, yank that sucker off, rip it up, and throw it away! Why should that person have to pay for that? See? You feel better already, don't you?

All joking aside, the best way to give to someone is without expectation that you will get something in return. The reward for giving or an act of kindness is a simple but powerful sense of joy. In fact, when I'm in the giving or kindness mode, I often get the lyrics of the late great Louis Armstrong stuck in my head: "And I say to myself, what a wonderful world."

A few years ago, I was having dinner alone at a wonderful restaurant at a hotel in Maui, Hawaii. It was a business expense, so don't give me a hard time. A couple in their thirties was dining a few tables away. I don't know what it was about them, but glancing their way I could see that they were completely engaged with each other, and it made me feel good. I overheard them talking to their waiter and discovered they were on their honeymoon. I watched as they held hands and gave thanks for the meal. Then they clinked their glasses softly and made a toast. I felt inspired by them and was moved by their obvious affection for each other.

As I finished my meal, I called the waiter over and told him that I wanted to pay for the couple's dinner. I billed their meal to my room and asked him to add a generous tip for himself. I also asked him not to reveal who paid the bill and handed him a note to give to them when they left. This is what the note said: "One could tell at first glance that you belong together. I wish you peace and joy."

The next morning I found a note on the floor by my door. It was from the waiter:

> Dear Mr. Rizzo,
>
> I believe what you did last night was a wonderful gesture, but you need to know the true impact you had on our newlyweds. When I told them that someone paid for their dinner, they were surprised to say the least. But when they read your note, they were overwhelmed with emotion. Then they explained why your note had such an effect.
>
> Our newlyweds are having a tough go of it at home. For reasons they didn't say, their families, including children from their previous marriages, are not too keen on them getting married. So, rather than having a wedding ceremony filled with people who really didn't want to be there, they decided to come to Maui to get married.
>
> They said that they made a toast and asked for a sign that they did the right thing. You, Mr. Rizzo, were the answer to their prayers. They said you confirmed, through divine guidance, what they already knew about each other. They asked me that if I ever saw you again, to please tell you, "Thank you! Thank you! Thank you for being their messenger of hope."

Growing up in New York I've been called a lot of things in my life, but never a messenger of hope. I liked the sound of it. One morning when Gina and I were walking the dogs around our property,

I told her I had been referred to as a "messenger of hope," and then I joked that I'd be shooting for sainthood next. Her reply was, "Okay, Saint Steven, but when you're done cleaning up the dog poop, go take out the garbage." Gina always has a way of keeping me grounded when I'm flying too high.

The point is that we all have opportunities to be messengers of hope when we give of ourselves and indulge in acts of kindness. These acts of kindness are spontaneous gestures that are driven by a sense of connection with other people and a realization that we're all dependent on each other as we go through life. It's really your higher self's way of reminding you that this is what life is all about. When you give of yourself, though, you are actually giving to yourself. It gives you a sense of hope in a world that sometimes seems hopeless.

Once I was at a departure gate at an airport in Dallas, waiting to go back home to New York. I was having a conversation with three Marines who had just returned from Iraq when the gate agent informed them that she had tried to get them an upgrade to first class but unfortunately there were no seats available. Flying coach was such a trivial concession that it was an easy decision to make. You should have seen the looks on all three Marines' faces when two other passengers and I gave up our first-class seats as a gesture of appreciation for their service. It goes without saying that the looks on those soldiers' faces were well worth giving up a little legroom, but you should have seen the look on our faces when we deplaned and saw all three Marines standing at attention saluting us!

Another way I give back is to make sure I always have extra copies of my books, DVDs, and CDs with me. I make it a habit to offer these tokens as gifts to someone who seems to be having a tough day or is giving me great service. The response I get in the way of e-mails and thank you letters puts everything in perspective, and is a great reminder of why I do what I do in the first place.

If you exhibit acts of kindness and show compassion to the people around you—family members, friends, business associates, and those you come in contact with every day—it will have a positive effect on both them and you. You may never know the outcome of the act as I happened to with the newlyweds, but you can be certain you are making a difference in a very positive way. Remember, what you give from your heart comes back to you in one way or another. Even though you may not feel it all the time, love is inside you. Let it out and witness your overall degree of happiness soar.

Make the activity of giving a habit. If you stay aware of the things around you, an opportunity will present itself. The next time you're feeling worried, take a look at the people around you and, trust me, an opportunity will arise. Take advantage of it, then notice how much better you feel.

There are many simple ways to give of yourself that can have a tremendous impact. The following are just a few examples of things you can do for someone else that take little or no effort and will surely brighten their day, if even for only a passing moment:

- Tell someone what a nice smile they have or how good they look.

- Give a salesman, customer service agent, or coworker a compliment for a job well done. Better yet, tell their superior!

- Write a letter or make a phone call to someone you haven't seen in a while and tell them you miss them.

- Buy a coffee for the person in line near you at the coffee shop.

- Let someone with only a few items move ahead of you while you're on line to check out at the supermarket.

- Ask someone if you can run an errand for them, even if it's out of your way.

- Remember the mailman, sanitation workers, gardeners, housekeepers, and others at holiday time.

- Take a moment to write a letter of praise to a company or organization for a great experience with their product or service. (This is also a great way to get free stuff!)

- Tell a child how special he or she is.

- Lend an ear to someone in need.

This list can go on forever, but you get the idea that every little thing counts. The extraordinary thing about giving is that it can become addictive. And this addiction won't lose you your job or get you evicted, unless you're in the habit of giving a little too much to your boss's or landlord's wife.

ATTITUDE ADJUSTMENT STRATEGY:
Practice giving and acts of kindness.

The reward you get from this habit is priceless. Practice this simple habit every day and you will feel your degree of overall happiness soar.

High Points to Remember

- Happiness is our main purpose and ultimate goal in life. All other goals, personally and professionally, are stepping-stones to happiness. In other words, you really want to achieve those goals because you believe they will make you happy or happier than you already are.

- If the process is polluted with negative energy and lack of enjoyment, it can only create more unhappiness when the outcome is achieved.

- Achievement does not make the person. The goal is just a gift. It's how you've lived and weathered the stormy seas of life that brings value to it.

- Your overall degree of happiness is determined by what you choose to focus on the most in the world day-to-day.

- Enjoyment is the spark that ignites passion and enthusiasm.

Part 3

May the Shift Be with You

Change your thoughts and change your world.

NORMAN VINCENT PEALE

In this section you will learn that it's not what happens to you that determines your quality of life, but how you *think* about what happens.

With practice you can learn to methodically shift your way of thinking and choose thoughts that will create a healthier belief system, make you feel better, and give you an optimistic attitude at work and in life.

You will also learn the magnificent effects humor and laughter can have in your life, especially when times are tough. Some of the stories that follow will show how humor literally nips negative thoughts in the bud, before they blossom into emotional havoc.

What You Think Is What You Get

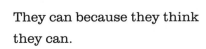

They can because they think
they can.

VIRGIL

I am amazed that some people have been given every advantage in life and still manage to sabotage their success and destroy their chances at happiness. Then there are those who seem to have every obstacle imaginable thrown in front of them and yet they still move ahead, refusing to give up. They take these obstacles and somehow manage to make their lives work and even enjoy the process as they go.

It is my belief that those in the latter group, consciously or unconsciously, shift their thoughts to create an empowering belief system that will steer them to a successful outcome. It's something of a Jedi mind shift, really. Use the force, intrepid reader. May the shift be with you.

If there is one thing I would love for you to walk away with after reading this section, it is the understanding that you have the power to experience any challenge in your life as a positive and an opportunity for growth. Notice I didn't say some challenges. I said any challenge. And the way that you ultimately experience these challenges is through the thought process. You identify, classify, and address all experiences through your continuous thoughts about them. Have you ever laid in bed and thought, "If only I could turn these thoughts off, I'd be able to get to sleep"? That's a testament to the constant presence of your inner monologue and its power.

Some people say that the challenging situations in life that are naturally presented to you dictate what kind of life you'll have. Others maintain that it's the way you react to these situations that determines your satisfaction in life. In my view, it's not the aggregate of your personal situations that determines your quality of life; rather, it's the way you think about them that governs their impact.

You can think of your thoughts as a conscious stream of mental judgments, evaluations, and even arguments. What's important to remember is that they are almost impossible to turn off, except perhaps through meditation. But even then those pain-in-the-butt thoughts will do whatever they can to keep you from the peace and quiet you deserve.

"Hello!" they'll say. "It's too quiet in here! I have things to say! What about my needs?"

Your thoughts can also be appraised in a very simple way: whether they strengthen or weaken you.

People who are successful tend to predominantly have thoughts of optimism for health, wealth, and abundance. Whether they are conscious of it or not, they simply don't allow negative thoughts of deficiency and failure to take root in their minds. That doesn't mean they don't have negative thoughts. We all do. It simply means that they're the people who see the glass half full, whose view of life is generally positive. It's easy to determine which kind or the other are the people you come into contact with. Have you noticed that those who dwell on their ailments are always ill? Those who speak about prosperity are prosperous. Those who talk about how wonderful life is are happy, and people who constantly talk about their cats, well, that's a different story. The point is that your thoughts cumulatively

provide a general blueprint of directives for how you react to everything in your life. Whatever you habitually think about or focus on
the most will appear in your life. So whatever you do, don't focus
on getting hit by a train. That's not going to end well. The following
story is a great example of the power of positive thinking.

His Claim to Fame: Eddie Murphy

One Saturday night in 1980, I was performing at East Side Comedy
Club on Long Island. I was fairly new in the comedy arena and this
was my first weekend appearance at a premier comedy club. To say
that I was a bit nervous would be an understatement. Sharing the
marquee with me was a young comic by the name of Eddie Murphy.
Yes, *the* Eddie Murphy. I knew Eddie pretty well back in the day. We
performed at a lot of one-night gigs together at bars, dance clubs,
and restaurants in the tristate area. Even though I was 12 years his senior, I knew from the moment I met Eddie that there was definitely
something special about him. He always stood out from everyone
else. Besides being brilliantly funny and having a great stage presence, he had an air of confidence on- and offstage that was unusual
for someone barely 18 years of age.

After the first show, Eddie and I were in the green room talking about what we wanted to do with our lives. At the time, I was
an English teacher during the day and a stand-up comedian at night
(although sometimes I had difficulty distinguishing between the
two). I told him my dream was to break into the comedy business in
a big way. Then Eddie said something to me that I will never forget.

"Steve," he said, "I'm going to be to comedy what the Beatles
were to music."

He didn't say, "I would like to be," or "My dream is to be." He
said it as if it were a matter of fact: "I'm going to be." He wasn't
bragging and it wasn't his ego getting carried away. There was no

conceit at all. His demeanor was calm and assertive. It was a simple statement that came from his heart; he said it with such conviction and utter certainty that I had no choice but to believe him.

Most people view Eddie Murphy's success at face value and think he became a big star simply because he was talented. Others think it was a matter of luck that Eddie was in the right place at the right time. Personally, I believe there was a lot more to Eddie Murphy's success than just talent and luck. In my view, the most powerful force at work in Eddie Murphy's rise to fame was the power of positive thinking.

I'm sure you'll agree that there are many extraordinarily talented people in all walks of life who never achieve the level of success they desire and/or deserve. You probably know a few personally. Have you ever wondered why? They seem to have what it takes to succeed, but somehow, for whatever reason, they never get that lucky break.

Back to Eddie Murphy. At that time in television history, the original cast of *Saturday Night Live* had retired and there was a search for a black comedian or actor with improvisational skills to replace Garrett Morris. A comedian was quickly chosen, but the producers discovered that this person unfortunately had difficulty reading and writing. So another, more urgent casting call was put out. At the time there were only a handful of black comedians, and Eddie was one of them. Auditions were being held at the Comic Strip in Manhattan, and as the story goes, within minutes of Eddie stepping onto the stage, the powers that be were convinced that he was going to be the newest player on *SNL*.

Now, you can call Eddie Murphy's rise to fame luck if you want to. But I believe we make our own luck. In other words, what you think is what you get. We manifest the things we desire in our lives with the power of our thoughts. If you are continuously creating positive thoughts and focusing your attention on the things you desire, if you take action with joy, passion, and enthusiasm and be-lieve without a doubt that it is just a matter of time before you achieve your desires, then more than likely that is exactly what will come to pass.

Take note that the key phrases to remember are "creating posi-tive thoughts," "taking action with joy, passion, and enthusiasm," and "believe without a doubt." I know. It's easier said than done. Don't give me that look. The good news, however, is that it can be done.

Eddie Murphy is a prime example of "what you think is what you get." I'm certain he achieved his level of success because he truly believed he was a star long before he became one. It was as if he had a crystal ball and saw how his life was going to unfold. It was just a matter of time before his determination to succeed would manifest in the physical world.

I witnessed firsthand how he carried himself on and off the stage. I had many heartfelt conversations with him. His focus on his craft was laser-sharp. His attitude was unfaltering. And his passion was second to none. He never drank alcohol or did drugs—never. His high was the joy he received from being onstage and making people laugh. I believe that Eddie Murphy radiated so much posi-tive energy and had such a powerful subconscious belief in himself that he attracted what we call lucky breaks into his life. He just hap-pened to have the talent and fortitude to take the appropriate action to seize opportunity when it knocked on his door.

What really separated Eddie Murphy from other talented co-medians, myself included, was that Eddie really, really wanted to be to comedy what the Beatles were to music. I mean, really! And he truly believed it was possible. When that combination of desire and belief comes together it is unstoppable. Eddie always knew where he was headed before he got there. More importantly, there was a con-stant correlation between his intention, his thoughts, and what was manifesting in his life.

The Bible says, "As a man thinketh so is he" (Proverbs 23:7). Many people refer to this as the "law of attraction." I'm from New York and I prefer the straightforward "What you think is what you get." It doesn't matter what you call it. All you need to know is that this spiritual law does not know good from bad, right from wrong, or true from false. It does not judge and it doesn't excuse negative thinking.

Early computer programmers came up with a nifty acronym to explain the occasional wrong results: GIGO. Pronounced "ghee-go," it stands for "garbage in, garbage out," and it refers to the fact that computers will unquestioningly process even the most non-sensical data inputted, inevitably spitting out erroneous information. The same is true of your thoughts. The results you receive are in direct accordance to what you're thinking. Like I said, "What you think is what you get." This powerful law will either make you or break you. Got it?

The great poet John Milton said, "The mind is its own place and it can make a heaven of hell or a hell of heaven." What a powerful statement and how true it is. The mind is its own place, but it's important that you understand that your thoughts both emanate from your mind and influence future thoughts that it generates. Those very thoughts are the determining factors that make a "heaven of hell" or a "hell of heaven" in your life.

Beliefs, Labels, and Writing the Stories of Your Life

Many of us hold on to the questionable truth that our belief system was influenced or even forced upon us when we were young by our parents, teachers, religious leaders, or whomever, and that we never really had a choice in the matter.

The fact is, unless you've been literally brainwashed, even if your beliefs were forced upon you by other people, they were still registered into your mind by way of your own thought process. So ultimately, now that you're an adult, on the most practical of levels, the original source is pretty inconsequential.

The point is that the beliefs you have about anything in your life are created by your constant thoughts. Imagine that your mind is a big cave, filled with different caverns. Your beliefs are truths that have been formed by a constant trickle of thoughts, depositing their positive, negative, and indifferent impressions, like stalactites and stalagmites, in your head. In one cavern are your beliefs about love, sex, marriage, children, and family; in another, about politics, religion, and your opinions of others. Like the unbelievable hairpiece your boss wears. Scattered throughout the cave are myriad formations that make up the positive, negative, and everything-in-between beliefs you have acquired, each being built from the slow, steady drip of your thoughts. Over time some beliefs seem set in stone and have become so huge that they are practically indestructible. Some are thin around the base and can crumble easily.

This mind-cave is a crude metaphor, but it illustrates how a constant trend in your thoughts can grow into beliefs. Sometimes that's a good thing. If your beliefs are shaped by positive streams of thought, you'll be left with positive beliefs that allow you to overcome, achieve, and succeed. If your brain is consistently bombarded by a barrage of toxic thoughts, a negative, self-limiting belief system is created and you can be crippled.

Now let's take this a step further. Your beliefs, whether good or bad, create the labels you wear. Your labels are the key factors that write the story of your life. Let me offer a personal example of how such a label influenced the course of my own life.

In 1992 I was sitting backstage at the Sands Hotel in Atlantic City. I had just finished the rehearsal for my Showtime comedy special that was to take place the following night. Woody Harrelson, who was hosting the show, approached me and asked me how I wanted to be introduced. I thought for a moment and said, "Tell them that you're going to bring in someone who was voted Least Likely to Succeed in his senior class in high school. Now he's here in Atlantic City at the Sands Hotel filming a Showtime special!" Yes, as I mentioned earlier, I was one of a number of students voted Least Likely to Succeed. Although the names on that list never made it into the yearbook, and at the time I took it as a big joke, the damage was still done.

Now I understand that it was that type of negative labeling that branded me and influenced the direction my life took. It instilled so much fear in me that it impeded my ability to move forward. My philosophy was, "If you don't try, you can't fail." This was the only way I knew how to avoid the rejection and failure I was convinced would result from anything I did. So I ignored or turned away from many opportunities. Even when I did push forward to make the effort, all it took was just one misstep or one criticism from someone in authority to reinforce the belief that I wasn't good enough.

These internal labels are created by the beliefs we have about ourselves and our surrounding world. They begin to form when we are children and for the most part are bestowed upon us by our parents, teachers, religious groups, and peers.

Of course we want to give the adults in our lives the benefit of the doubt and assume their intentions were good, but nonetheless the results may have been devastating. Children are vulnerable to the opinions and thoughts of others. Some labels are programmed into a young mind by a dominating parent who never gave the child a chance to think for herself. "I know what's best for you." "You listen to me." "I know what will make you happy." Others may have been told by a teacher that they simply weren't smart enough or good enough to fulfill their dream. "I don't think you're cut out for this. Why don't you try something else?"

Whatever the messages you received when you were young, by the time you were an adult they became your reality and the labels you wear. You might be wearing a positive label that signifies that you are smart and have the confidence to meet any challenge. That's your brand and you carry it with you everywhere you go. You might be wearing a toxic label that signifies you are incapable of making wise decisions. That too is your brand and it will have some influence in every decision you make. Either way, labels represent who you *think* you are. Your labels, good or bad, are the determining factors for the choices you make and the actions you take.

Whether positive or negative, your labels are the foundation of your life. Your success and happiness are built upon them. If your foundation is comprised of fear, anger, self-doubt, a feeling of hopelessness and being overwhelmed, the label you wear is toxic. Nothing can distort the way you view your life and your surrounding world more than toxic labels. They have the power to paralyze you physically, mentally, emotionally, and spiritually.

Toxic labels can take control of your life when your past emotional experiences are triggered in a present situation. When I was a child, I grew up listening to my parents arguing about money and paying the bills. There never seemed to be enough money. In fact, financial issues were a source of frequent arguments and conflict in my home. Eventually I absorbed my parents' fears about money and carried those negative labels into my adult life. Even now, when I have financial security, I still feel I have to be on guard when those notions of financial scarcity are triggered in a current-day situation.

Whether positive or negative, the labels you've placed on yourself have an impact on how you react to the day-to-day circumstances that make up your daily life. That reality then becomes the story of your life. The more you hold on to the stories created by the negative labels you wear, the more you validate the false reality they represent. This continuing cycle has a profound effect on your destiny, both personally and professionally.

That said, it's important to understand that your personal circumstances are made up of the string of events that occur in your life. It's what you do or how you choose to respond to these events that determines how your story is written. Once you seize control and challenge the negative labels you carry, your life circumstances change. Labels do not write your story, you do. You are the author of your own story. You decide how it will be written when you choose to experience the events in your life in any given way.

What is your personal truth? Are you grateful for what you have, or are you resentful and bitter about what is lacking? Do you feel blessed? Do you feel cursed? Do you learn from your mistakes and move forward with confidence, or do you berate yourself and quit for fear of failing? Are you the victor or the victim? Do you savor and enjoy the moment, or do you live by the clock and believe you just don't have time to laugh and enjoy the process? I think you get my point. If not, I'm sorry, I just can't think of any more examples. If you can come up with a few more, feel free to include them.

How you answer all of these questions creates the beliefs that shape how you experience your life. Stop and ask yourself, "Am I writing a story of abundance and joy? Or am I writing a story of scarcity and despair?" It is sad indeed to watch naturally gifted people who have every advantage and possibility of success strip themselves of empowerment. Bad habits and years of negative reinforcement create a belief system that convinces them that they are not good enough, worthy enough, smart enough, fortunate enough, and a host of other "not enoughs" that cause them to foil their own dreams and sabotage their own happiness.

This entire conditioning process and the reinforcing of bad mental habits are fueled by negative self-talk. I call it "self-curse-talk," because this type of internal dialogue literally curses you with its power to cast a spell on your life.

Stop Cursing Your Life!

Let's say our friend Bernie wants to take his business to the next level. Yes, Bernie is back (as if he had a choice), and he wants to achieve this goal more than anything else, but like all business ventures, there's a certain amount of risk. So he does all the research and gathers all the information he needs to begin working toward his goal. Bernie is psyched and filled with enthusiasm. He honestly believes that nothing can stop him.

Then somewhere along the way to his goal, Bernie encounters some unexpected obstacles and things don't look as promising as they did when he started. He's having trouble getting a permit he needs and an office expansion is going to cost double the original estimate. Soon his enthusiasm turns to frustration, and this frustration turns into self-doubt, worry, and fear.

It isn't long before Bernie's inner dialogue morphs into something like this: "I knew this would happen. Every time I go for something big, it never works out! What was I thinking? I must have been out of my mind to think I could do this!"

Blah blah blah, yada yada yada. Congratulations, Bernie, you've just entered the Negative Zone. The Negative Zone is worse than the Dead Zone and the Twilight Zone put together. Think of it as a No Parking Zone for your hopes and dreams.

How much progress will Bernie make toward his goal with this type of inner dialogue? The sad truth is that many people who think and talk like this are clueless as to the impact it has on their quality of life. They have no idea that by allowing negative thoughts to dominate, they are opening the way for more feelings of hopelessness and defeat. Those very thoughts are creating or reinforcing existing subconscious beliefs that are keeping them from what they desire. They just don't understand that what they think is what they get.

This is self-curse-talk. If there is anything that can keep you from being productive and partaking in the abundance that life has to offer, it's self-curse-talk. If you have a tendency to believe that a tough situation is worse than what it is, it's self-curse-talk. If you're wondering why you're not enjoying the journey of your life, it's self-curse-talk. And if you find yourself more often in a state of unhappiness than happiness, it could very well be because of chronic self-curse-talk.

Self-curse-talk comes from relating your current situation with some past experience. If your thought process is like our friend Bernie's, whenever you've tried to succeed at something, either you haven't been able to shake off past failures or you've been afraid of being unable to match the previous levels of success you've achieved. You compare past failure with your current situation or try to convince yourself that wins in the past were a fluke. The good news is, if you can recognize your self-curse-talk for what it really is—nothing more than unnecessary baggage from your past that you carry into the present by way of your own thinking—then you can choose to gradually shift your way of thinking to create thoughts, words, and beliefs that will make you feel better and put you in a better position to achieve success.

The thing to understand about self-curse-talk is that it reflects your internalized negative feelings about yourself rather than an empirical truth. In other words, just because you feel it doesn't make it true. Just because you say it to yourself does not make it true. But if you believe that it is true, that's all that matters in your world. That brain of yours (or your subconscious) does not know the difference between true and false. It cannot make independent judgments and instead understands your thoughts to be what they are—just thoughts. If you do not recognize and squash a negative thought when it pops up, your subconscious takes it as truth, thus compounding and affirming that negative feeling and further solidifying a belief system that will have negative consequences.

As I discussed earlier, the morning is the time of day that sets the tone for the next 24-hour cycle. Allowing one negative thought to go unchallenged first thing in the morning can cause a snowball effect that influences everything you do throughout the day. One negative thought can take an otherwise promising day and blow it to pieces. Isn't it amazing how no outside help is necessary to ruin your day? Didn't think you were that powerful, did you?

Not only can self-curse-talk ruin a promising day, it can also destroy an entire life of promise. Many gifted and talented people don't achieve their goals or fulfill their potential because they keep hearing and replaying the same recording in their heads over and over again:

"This just isn't going to work."

"I just don't have the money and never will."

"I'm not lucky."

"I better play it safe."

"I can't believe how stupid I am."

"This happens every time I try to improve my life!"

The spell has been cast, and the culprit is—you guessed it!—self-curse-talk. This type of thinking amounts to self-sabotage, and usually people either do it or they don't. People who have the proclivity for self-curse-talk use this type of thinking in virtually everything they do, empowering an already negative belief system and solidifying toxic labels that influence the unfolding story of their lives.

The bottom line is this: the power of your beliefs is immense. It can lift you up and take you to the highest highs or drag you down to the lowest lows. Eddie Murphy believed he was a star before he became one. Rodney Dangerfield put his happiness on hold, believing he couldn't be fulfilled until he became a star. Whether positive or negative, your beliefs create the reality that guarantees your success or failure.

Okay. Now we've established the connection between your thoughts and beliefs. But there's more! Not only do your thoughts create your beliefs, they also create your emotional reality. To illustrate this point, let's do a little experiment.

Right now I want you to try feeling angry, but do it without thinking about anything that makes you angry. It doesn't work, right? How can you feel angry without thinking about something that elicits that emotion from you? You can't. It's impossible. Now try feeling guilty without thinking about something specific that you feel guilty about. Once again, you can't. The thought has to come first. Your emotional state is also the direct result of your thoughts. And the tone of your thoughts becomes your life experience.

Now you may be thinking, "Okay, so what you're telling me is that all I have to do is keep a tab on my thoughts throughout the day and everything will be fine." Sorry, that's not how it works. It's impossible to monitor all of your thoughts. Researchers say that each of us has over 60,000 thoughts a day. My head hurts just thinking about that.

Since being conscious of every thought you have is impossible, there's an easy way to help you determine if you're doing yourself subconscious damage. View your feelings as an emotional warning system. When you're feeling good and happy, you must be thinking good thoughts. When you're feeling bad and crappy, you must be thinking bad thoughts. When you change your thoughts, you change the way you feel, and when you change the way you feel, you change your life experience.

Your emotions are the broadcasting signals that let you know if you are on track to get what you want. So whenever you're feeling bad or in a low mood, you're sending signals to bring more bad stuff your way. If you don't make an effort to tune in to this process and change your thoughts and feel better, you're telling yourself that it's okay to continue to feel bad and you're laying welcome to a bad mood. And that's exactly what you'll get.

The Snowball Effect

Let's break down step-by-step how self-curse-talk works and can "snowball" out of control. We'll use an example of someone being delayed at an airport. I wonder who that someone would be. Sorry, Bernie. I'm not trying to pick on you, but you make such a great example.

Our friend Bernie is at an airport on his way to a very important business meeting when an announcement is made that his flight is canceled. Bernie moves to the end of a long line of people trying to get to the ticket agent to book the next flight out. To make matters worse, there is only one airline representative trying to accommodate everyone. (Oh gee, what else is new?) The line seems to be at a complete standstill. Then it happens. Bernie shakes his head in disgust and blurts out, "Here we go again!"

That's it. That's all it takes. The spell has been cast. Let the curse begin. Bernie has just opened the door to the Negative Zone. It opened the moment he shook his head and said the magic words, "Here we go again!" He is now vulnerable and defenseless. That one statement and the negative resolve behind it might seem like no big deal. Who hasn't expressed frustration in a situation like that?

However, it is the one little pebble shifting that leads to an avalanche of similar, more dangerous thoughts.

"This is absolutely ridiculous! I just can't depend on this airline anymore. In fact, I can't depend on anyone anymore! If they cared they'd have more people trying to accommodate us. Why do I give them my business anyway? Now I'm going to lose the account because I'll be late. I'm probably wasting my time anyway."

In a matter of seconds, Bernie takes this experience to another level. I mean, it's bad enough that he's stuck at the airport. But now he actually begins to believe that everyone is out to get him and he's wasting his time because he won't have success with his client anyway.

"Look at this guy! What an idiot. Doesn't he know he should have his ID ready before he gets to the counter? No wonder this line isn't moving. No one knows what the hell they're doing! I wish this kid would shut up. If parents can't control their children they shouldn't bring them to the airport! Why is it that every time I'm in line somewhere I'm surrounded by idiots?"

It's obvious that this cycle of negative thinking is showing Bernie no mercy. Not only is the door to the Negative Zone open, but he is being sucked in. At this point he is well on his way to believing that every aspect of his life is in total chaos.

"This is ridiculous! Oh great, it's raining! Now I'll never get out of here. What else is going to happen? What a way to make a living! If that's what you want to call it."

Now Bernie's emotional state is completely out of whack with reality and his body has started to tense up. Here is where he goes in for the kill and destroys any chance of coming to grips with his exaggerated experience of what has happened:

"Why do I go through all of this aggravation? I make all of this money for what? So the IRS can take half! And half of the half I have left goes right back into my business! What good is making money if I can't enjoy it? I spend most of my time in traffic, airports, airplanes, and hotels! This is absolutely insane." (Yes, it is. I'm an emotional wreck just writing this.)

It's clear that our friend Bernie has set himself up for a miserable day and then some. He's allowed his thoughts on this brief setback to lead him to believe that his life isn't working. He's actually convinced himself that he's miserable. Of course, this is causing him to have a really bad attitude, one that leaves him feeling hopeless and drained, and will no doubt lead him to take action that will lead to an outcome that he'll regret. Pretty depressing, huh? And it all started with one little thought. "Here we go again," indeed. Obviously, Bernie doesn't have his shift together.

There are people out there who think like this on a continual basis, in all facets of their lives, and if you think you might be one of them, it is time to seize the moment and do something about it. Bernie couldn't get a handle on his situation because he didn't think to pick up a copy of this book. But you're already reading it, so you've got a real shot at getting your shift together!

Methodically Shift Your Thoughts

How do we break away from the tired treadmill of our "woe is me" stories? How do we keep ourselves from feeling victimized every time some situation in our lives doesn't turn out the way we want it to? First of all, you have to become aware of what you are doing to yourself. You can't remedy a negative situation such as Bernie's if you're not aware of what you are doing to yourself and its consequences. You have to understand that your thoughts and emotions are caught up in a vicious cycle that is causing you to veer out of control.

Once you recognize that this is your MO, you've arrived at a good place and a window of opportunity. Now you can methodically shift your way of thinking and choose thoughts that will gradually make you feel better, in the moment and for the long term. This is not a "snap yourself back into a good mood" process. It's not about going instantly from an emotionally distraught state to a joyful one. That's just not possible—your brain would probably pop.

The key word to remember is "gradual." It is a thought-by-thought process that gradually makes you feel better and better, until finally you've calmed your nervous system down and you can view the situation at hand from a higher perspective. Bernie was caught up in a whirlwind of negative drama. Not only were his negative thoughts building and feeding off each other, but the longer he focused on what was not working, the more power he gave them. You could say that Bernie, the poor guy, was on a negative rampage. And this rampage was causing him to feel totally helpless and out of control.

In a way, there may be some level of comfort in feeling helpless sometimes, that no matter what you do, you can't win. After all, if you believe the world is conspiring against you, you don't have to take responsibility for your unhappiness. But that perspective will lead you nowhere fast.

If at some point in his meltdown Bernie were to become aware of what he was doing to compound a bad situation, if he were to acknowledge that his negativity was feeding upon itself, and if he were to come to understand the consequences of remaining in that emotional state, he could then choose to methodically shift his way of thinking and create thoughts that will make him feel better. (You go, Bernie!)

"Wow, I have to calm down. I'm making this worse than it really is. I have a meeting today. It's important that I'm in the right frame of mind. I know from past experience that being irate and upset won't get me what I want. The cancellation is really out of my control. So is the weather. So is that kid that won't shut up. The good news is that I was smart enough to get here early and I have enough time to catch another flight. That poor ticket agent is doing the best she can. When it's my turn, I'll do it with a smile and understanding. Not only does she need a break, but so do I. I can handle this."

Does that sound like the most unrealistic inner dialogue ever? Maybe. But just one of those thoughts could be enough to get the situation under control. This shift in thinking will actually bring Bernie to solutions to the current situation. The more he attempts to create positive thoughts, the more positive his reality will become. Even the slightest shift in thinking will give him a feeling of relief and start him on his way to finding a solution. Looks like Bernie is turning into a real shift-head!

If you find yourself in a situation that is triggering a negative rampage like Bernie's, you must stop, take a breath, and remind yourself that your habitual negative thought patterns distort the reality of what is happening. When you realize that you have a choice as to how you view any given situation, you can then take actions to feel better. Once you start to feel better, a brighter outcome will prevail. When you acknowledge your experience and the change that occurred because of the different actions you took, you have taken one more step in the process of building the happy life you want. But seriously, folks, get a handle on your kids at the airport. Please, for Bernie's sake!

The Eeyore Syndrome

I know a woman, a full-time resident of the Negative Zone, who saved for years to go on her dream vacation. Once she got there, it rained constantly and her holiday was ruined. Now, it's important to understand that residing in the Negative Zone means that no matter what good may come your way, you will find something wrong with it. This is what I call the Eeyore Syndrome. You remember A. A. Milne's classic character, Eeyore. This friend of Winnie the Pooh was a threadbare gray donkey that was always moping around, talking to himself and awaiting his inevitable misfortune.

Well, that's this woman. I swear she could win $500 million in the lottery and her attitude would be, "Oh boy. I just knew this would happen. Now the government is going to take half and I'll wind up with only $250 million. Why does everything have to happen to me?"

She's the kind of person you want to smack right in the back of the head and shout, "Snap out of it!" In fact, I think there should be a law that permits us to do just that. We'll call it the Whiny Law. It should establish our right to approach anyone who is whining and smack them right in the back of the head. Not to hurt them (not a lot, anyway), but just enough to snap them out of it. If you're a whiner, watch out if I ever run for public office.

When this woman came back from her vacation, she couldn't wait to tell me everything that went wrong. I got comfortable and let her vent her woes.

"Oh my God, Steven," she said despairingly. "Do you know how long we saved for this vacation? And you've known me long enough to know that if something is going to happen to anyone, chances are it will happen to me! It's been that way ever since I was a child. Can you believe it rained every day while we were on our vacation? I should have realized something like this would happen! Why would I expect anything else? My brother went on vacation last year and he and his girlfriend had a wonderful time! My sisters just came back two weeks ago from their vacations with their families and everyone was so nice and tan. But no, not us! The weather was horrible from the day we arrived to the day we left." Shaking her head in sorrow, she said, "The rain ruined our vacation!"

She looked at me for sympathy, but all I could think of was how much I wished the Whiny Law was in effect.

Let's get this straight. The rain didn't ruin this woman's vacation. What really ruined it was the constant bombardment of negative thinking that caused her to feel victimized. It was her thoughts about the bad weather that supported an overwhelmingly negative belief system and a preexisting bad attitude that ruined her vacation. Yes, of course, it would have been nice if she had had some sunshine on the trip. But she didn't. And in concentrating so much of her energy on what wasn't working, she never gave herself a chance to have a good time. It's impossible to have a good time or a successful outcome if your thoughts are causing you to be miserable. Okay, now you can take the blue-sky-and-clouds metaphor literally.

When you allow outside circumstances to determine your happiness, your natural state of peace deteriorates. When this happens, inner peace is replaced with a feeling that you are being cheated. That's how you get caught up in the Eeyore Syndrome.

"Why is it that every time I get in line at a grocery store, there's a price check?"

"Why does it have to rain now?"

"Why can't I get a break?"

"My life really sucks."

"I should have stayed in bed."

"This will never work."

"Who am I kidding anyway?"

This type of thinking reflects a lack of confidence in yourself and a failure to trust in the process of life. As a result, your enjoyment and appreciation of all the good stuff that life has to offer gets distorted, leaving you in a victimized state and an ultimately unhappy existence. Remember, thoughts don't just happen. They are something we create and therefore we are able to direct them. When something upsetting happens, it's your thoughts about the situation that will either minimize or magnify the effect it will have on you.

My friend allowed herself to create a thought pattern that was causing a negative emotional response and was setting off an unhealthy physical response. You don't need to be a doctor to know that her heart was racing, her stomach was tight, and she simply wasn't feeling right. Those physiological side effects were causing her to think even more negatively, which in turn agitated her condition, and so on and so forth. It was a vicious cycle that she was creating. In fact, the real absurdity in all this is that this woman will relive the entire ordeal of her rainy vacation every time she tells this story, multiplying her negativity far more than the actual experience ever could— a classic example of the snowball effect. And I'm willing to bet that she has an arsenal of similar woe-is-me stories to prove to the world and to herself that she was, and always will be, a victim.

So instead of whining and making statements about how bad things are and how bad things have been, make every attempt to make statements that cause you to see the situation from a more positive angle. The choice is yours. You can choose to become the victim or the victor. That's why the habit of methodically shifting your thoughts is paramount. Remember, the goal to bouncing back from any negative experience is to find ways to make yourself feel better.

Let's look at another example of how this works. What happens when you lose your cool and get into an argument with someone? What are the repercussions if you hold on to your anger? Letting go of the anger and dealing constructively with whatever has upset you is the right choice 100 percent of the time. How do you do that? By recognizing your feelings and making the appropriate choices to rectify the situation, beginning with creating thoughts that will ultimately lift you up and make you feel better so you can think clearly about how to handle things.

Say to yourself, "Okay, I blew it, but I need to bounce back from this."

"I can't take this mood with me throughout the day."

"I need an attitude adjustment."

"I have to get my shift together."

"This is not about who is right or wrong. It's about ego and relationship advantages. I'll apologize for losing my temper."

"I like knowing I'm in control of how I feel."

"I've already made up my mind. I promised myself that I will enjoy the day, and I'm going to."

"I choose to be happy now."

If you're berating yourself for making a mistake at work or for falling short of achieving a goal, consider the consequences if you continue to beat yourself up about it. Remind yourself to focus on your number one priority, which is to be happy.

Say to yourself, "Okay, I vented. Now that that's out of my system, I need to bounce back."

"Okay, it's time to get my shift together."

"Okay, I'm being too hard on myself. I will only feel worse if I continue to beat myself up over this."

"Okay, I better adjust my attitude."

"Okay, I can figure this out. I'm good at figuring things out."

"Okay, I'm going to learn from this and start over."

"Okay, I have far too many things going for me to quit now."

"Okay, I promised myself I will enjoy this entire process, and that's what I'm going to do."

"Okay, I choose to be happy now."

You may have noticed that each of those scenarios began with saying, "Okay," followed by a reflection on how to defuse the situation. When analyzing negative thoughts so that you can begin to methodically shift to more positive ones, a good place to start is with a deep breath and saying to yourself, "Okay," then go on from there. Okay?

"I'm talking to you, okay. Answer me!"

"Okay."

Same Scenario, Different Outcome

To illustrate how your attitude affects your experience of any given situation, let me tell you about another couple's vacation. Like the couple you just met, these two also had bad weather, but on top of that two of their flights were canceled, one was delayed, and when they finally landed, the airline cheerfully announced that they could not locate their luggage. Yet the couple came back home with reports of what a great time they had. How did this couple manage to salvage and enjoy their vacation while the woman with the Eeyore Syndrome had a disaster of a holiday? The answer is that this couple was on drugs. In fact, they weren't even on vacation. They were so high at home in their living room that they only thought they were. Just kidding! Sometimes I just can't help myself. It's the comedian in me. The real answer is that this smart, self-aware couple methodically steered their thoughts to create a brighter outcome.

I asked Charlie, the husband in the second couple, if he experienced any upset at all about these unfortunate circumstances. He told me that he vented his frustration and let the airline know how unhappy he was about the entire situation. I then asked him what turned it around. He thought about it and replied, "Well, after waiting in the airline terminal on and off for three days we were pretty numb. When we were finally boarding the plane I looked at Sara and said, 'We have to snap out of this mood! We're still on vacation. Okay, three days were spent at the airport, but we still have five days left. Yes, the weather doesn't look very promising, but we can still have a good time! We can turn this around. We have to! We'll make new plans. We'll go to the resort and ask them what excursions are available in the rain.' Then Sara jumped in on my enthusiasm and reminded me that we needed some romantic time together and this would be a good time to do it. Then we laughed together at her choice of words."

Before long, Charlie and Sara were cracking jokes and found themselves laughing at the entire situation. They even laughed at the lost luggage. The airline said they would reimburse them for a shopping spree if their luggage was not delivered later that day. "Hey, great!" they thought. "We'll go shopping at the airline's expense and probably get our luggage the next day."

The moment Charlie and Sara became aware of the negative state they were in, they made a conscious choice to shift their thoughts from the problem to the opportunity it represented, and they began to feel better. They also made empowering statements that helped to lift their spirits, setting the stage for creativity and a positive outcome. These actions, plus their capacity to find the courage to laugh despite their disappointment, powered their ability to view the entire ordeal as an adventure rather than a crisis. When Charlie and Sara came back from vacation, they were able to talk about what a great time they had.

It's easy to play the victim. It's easy to blame outside circumstances for interfering with your plans and goals. There are a host of convenient scapegoats for your life not going exactly the way you want: the weather, the economy, your spouse, your job, your boss, the government, nature, your zipper, or even God (God forbid). It can be difficult to take responsibility for your success and happiness, yet that is exactly what you must do.

When things aren't going your way and everything seems to be falling apart around you, immediately stop complaining. It only makes matters worse and in reality is a real beatdown for the people around you. Instead, use my friends Charlie and Sara as an example. Look for something good that might come of your circumstances. Sometimes you have to push yourself to see the bright side. It's really not that difficult. It's not brain surgery, but more like a brain adjustment. Remember: what you think is what you get. If you can't see the bright side, then step away from the situation for a while and focus your attention on something that will lift you up, like your children, your dog or cat, or that funny yet profound book you just read. Or get involved in some kind of activity that makes you feel good, such as walking or exercising, or take time for a funny movie or just to enjoy the scenery. The goal is simply to get back to feeling good. Build on those feelings and go from there.

Every minute that you wallow in a negative state, you keep yourself from the quality of life you desire. Instead, consciously and methodically shift your thoughts, and little by little your negativity will diminish. Be consistent and methodical in your approach and you will feel the difference as you gradually continue to reject negative thoughts and replace them with an empowering way of thinking. You will begin to respond to challenging situations from a position of faith and hope for the future, rather than fear, and as such you will quite naturally come to expect good things instead of bad. The choice is yours and it always has been. It's up to you to make the right choice for your own happiness.

ATTITUDE ADJUSTMENT STRATEGY:
Methodically shift your thoughts.

Once you recognize that your thoughts are causing your emotions to snowball out of control, methodically shift your way of thinking and choose thoughts that will gradually make you feel better. If you can master this habit, you can master your life.

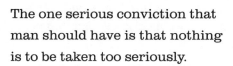

Humor: The Instant Mind Shift

8

> The one serious conviction that
> man should have is that nothing
> is to be taken too seriously.
>
> **SAMUEL BUTLER**

We're living in a world that's moving incredibly fast. On top of our personal problems and everyday pressures, the newspapers and evening newscasts tell us that our economy is falling apart, corporations are being forced to downsize, and massive technological advances are causing people to reevaluate, adjust, and change their lives. Cell phones, BlackBerries, iPhones, and tablet devices, e-mails, text messages, and even micro-communication applications like Twitter are clogging our minds with an overwhelming amount of information, leaving us with little or no time to relax, unwind, and focus our attention on the big picture.

To compound this, political unrest, crime, disease, prejudice, and violence are running rampant, as they've done for centuries. Hold on a second. I need to take a break here. I'm getting depressed. I'll be right back.

Okay, I'm back now. Where was I? Oh yeah, I remember. The divorce rate is at an all-time high; despite an unwilling public, war seems to be the number one strategy for dealing with conflict between nations; and at any moment we could be the target of a terrorist attack. It's really no wonder why so many of us have to be medicated in some way or another in order to cope with the madness our civilization has created!

We all need ways to reduce the tension and deal with the fast pace that we are subjected to every day. I honestly believe that our ability to shift and occasionally laugh off the major and minor tensions in our lives is crucial in order for us to survive the insanity. I'm not just suggesting this, I'm telling you. We *have* to take time out of each day and laugh. Why do you think people go to comedy clubs, watch sitcoms, and see funny movies? Because they want to laugh. Why do they want to laugh? For the same reason that they want to have sex: it simply makes them feel good. A physiological and mental reaction takes place when you laugh. Laughter charges your inner battery and helps you cope with tough times. Even if you are having a really bad day, when you laugh, life doesn't seem that bad after all.

This is why I urge you to unleash the power of your Humor Being on a daily basis. Right now you're probably wondering, "Great, Steve. I'll do that. But what is a 'Humor Being'?" That, I can explain.

Let me start off by saying that I believe that everyone on this planet is born with their own internal Humor Being. Unfortunately, some people live their entire lives without ever knowing they have this powerful gift within them, let alone how to tap into it and make it work for them.

Before describing the characteristics of a Humor Being, let me first define what a sense of humor is. The dictionary says the word *sense* means "perception or awareness; and correct reasoning; or sound judgment." The word *humor* means "turn of mind; to sooth temper or mood, or the mental quality that produces absurd or joyful ideas." So we can say by definition that a "sense of humor" means to be aware that you have a mental quality to turn your mind in an unusual way, or a need to produce joyful or absurd ideas that can soothe your very being. The initiative and proficiency with which you utilize your sense of humor, however, comes from what I call your Humor Being.

Your Humor Being is part of your higher self. It's the part of you that brings out the best of who you are when times get tough. What your Humor Being gives you more than anything else is emotional stability and peace of mind. Making a habit of invoking your Humor Being will turn you into a happier person with a brighter outlook.

Tapping into your Humor Being is one of the tools that can help you cope with the natural ups and downs of life. Instead of going through life allowing unfortunate situations, unlucky circumstances, and foul people to suck the energy right out of us, we can turn to our Humor Being for a levity break. As the stories in this book show, those who make the shift and live in harmony with their Humor Being have the ability to see the bright side of a negative situation. They embrace change more easily and make conscious choices to enjoy themselves during the process of whatever they are trying to achieve.

As we discussed earlier, our natural state is that of joy and inner peace. It's our responsibility to stay connected to that state each and every day, and it's our Humor Being's job to help us maintain that connection. After all, humor is one of the qualities that make us human, so why not use it?

My parents taught me four important things about life: You have to be proud of who you are. You have to be proud of where you're from. You have to be proud of what you do for a living. And you need a sense of humor about all three. I will take that with me until the day I die.

My entire family has a great sense of humor. Humor was the one thing that helped us through the tough times. However, I believe my mom and dad were at their funniest when they weren't trying to be, especially when they were arguing. Like the first time I used the family car and got into an accident. This of course was right after my father had given me the big lecture. "Look at me," he said. (I could never understand why he always said that to me, as if looking at him was going to make me hear better.) "This is the only car this family has! Don't get into an accident!" Well, I wasn't planning on it, but since he planted the thought in my head, that's all I could think of. And as you already know, what you think is what you get.

I remember calling from a pay phone, praying that my mother would answer the phone. "Mom, I got into an accident!" I said. "Oh my God!" she said. "Are you okay?" I felt instant relief that her only concern was about my welfare. Then I heard my father's voice screaming out from the background. "How's the car?" That's when the argument started. My mother said, "Your son just got into an accident! Who cares about the car?" My father's reply: "Hey, we have three sons and one car!" And the argument continued.

Humor Being to the Rescue

The first time I can recall my Humor Being having a dramatic effect on my life was when I was in the third grade. I was performing in the play version of *Alice in Wonderland*. No, I wasn't Alice. I was Humpty Dumpty. You know, the egghead who was damaged irreparably when he found out he didn't have workers' compensation. It was opening night and the auditorium was packed with parents, teachers, students, and their families. Peering out from the wings of the stage, I could see the rows of expectant faces. That's a lot of pressure for a third grader. The time for my scene came in the blink of an eye. There I was, sitting on the wall in my egg costume. Everything was going fine until my line, "I'm one who has spoken to a king, I am!" Well, I guess I said it with just a little too much enthusiasm, because I lost my balance and fell over the back side of the wall. All the audience could hear was a giant thud! I didn't get hurt (not physically, anyway). But I remember how humiliated I felt waiting behind that wall for the house to realize that falling wasn't a part of the act just yet. All I could think of was that I had messed up big time. I was going to be the laughingstock of the entire school. I thought the rest of the cast would berate me for ruining the play. "And how," I wondered, "can I ever face my parents?" I wanted to run off the stage and hide, but I was frozen by fear, crouching behind the wall, an egg with egg on his face.

While the negative thoughts were running rampant in my mind, the teacher in charge was running up the steps from the first row and calling out, "Steven, are you okay?" It was instinct to rely on the ability that had gotten me out of bad situations before: humor. Without missing a beat I yelled out as loud as I could, "Yeah! But I think I cracked my shell. I hope Alice doesn't mind scrambled eggs!" To my young surprise, the entire audience exploded with laughter. Hearing the laughter, I slowly stuck my head above the wall to check out what was going on. As soon as they saw my big egg head, the laughter turned into cheers and everyone in that auditorium, including the cast, was standing and chanting, "Hump-ty! Hump-ty!" Because scrambled eggs just aren't as good without a little ham, I jumped on top of the wall and proceeded to take many exaggerated bows. The teacher was begging me to please sit down before I fell off again, but I couldn't help myself. I was totally blown away by the reaction and attention I was getting. The cheers and the laughter grew louder as I took one final bow. Eventually I sat down and the play continued and was a huge success. What happened that night that allowed me to shift from embarrassing failure to incredible success? My Humor Being came to the rescue.

In a matter of seconds there was a major shift in perspective. Just by blurting out the first obvious joke that came to my mind, I went from a klutz to a hero. An emotional transformation took place. The situation went from the most humiliating experience in my young life to becoming the star of the show. And I'm not exaggerating when I say "star." When the play was over, I was actually signing autographs. Now that's what I call getting my shift together!

How would my life story have changed if I had allowed fear to be the dominating factor that night? Would there have been a stand-up career without that fall? Would I be motivated today to speak to hundreds of audiences a year about the importance of adopting a positive attitude?

Every time I look back on this significant incident in my life I am reminded of how important it is to be in control of my emotions and how laughter can help me take that control. It doesn't matter how old you are or what kind of position in life you hold. When you make the shift and find the laughter in the midst of any stressful situation, you can regain control. As I said earlier when I described the tollbooth incident, when you make that shift to humor, your brain is no longer registering negative thoughts that cause you to be upset. In fact, your brain has switched gears and is focusing on what made you laugh. Even if your brain does go back to whatever it was that was upsetting, you won't feel as overwhelmed as you were before. Why? Because in addition to signaling to yourself that your problem is laughable, you've also stopped the rampage of negative thinking. You've calmed your nervous system down to the point where you can shift your thoughts and think clearly, reassess the situation, bounce back, and take control. That night as Humpty Dumpty, when I joined in with the laughter of the audience, I felt instant relief. I regained my confidence, took control, and bounced right back up onto that wall.

Our Inner Conflicts

It's no coincidence that we are confronted with annoying people and situations day in and day out. That's life and it follows you everywhere, like someone stepping on your heels. When we allow these outside factors to keep us from enjoying our lives, they become internalized and manifest themselves as inner conflicts. Make no doubt about it, those inner conflicts represent lessons we need to learn. When we learn them we nourish the soul and become more confident and at peace with our surroundings. Our lives become easier when we view our challenges not as burdens that bring us down, but as opportunities to raise us up.

Among my biggest challenges has been to learn patience and to control my anger. I often find myself in traffic jams, stuck at red lights, and waiting at the back of long lines. This last one seems to be especially true. No matter what line I carefully choose for optimal speed, factoring in the number of standees, the number of their items, and whether or not they look like they have someplace else to be, something always comes up in the way of a price check, changing the cash drawer, a dysfunctional computer (or person), or a declined credit card. This is maddening to me, but I firmly believe that until I accept that I don't have the power to make lines move faster, I will continue to find myself in these situations.

It seems like whenever I'm in a hurry to get somewhere, anything can happen, and it usually does. I can't tell you how often I notice a stain on my shirt or a broken shoelace. Sometimes I can't find my car keys or I notice the gas tank is near empty. Boy, does life seem stupid sometimes.

If I allow even one of these annoying moments to try my patience, it could set me off for the rest of the day. In the end, all it takes is one annoyance to influence another one, and then another, and so on. This domino effect can be devastating, but when I recognize it for what it is and say to myself, "This is a test, and I will pass it and learn from it," I set myself up for a happier, more productive day. Here's where humor can really be a difference maker.

One time, Gina and I were running late for an important dinner engagement with a corporate client and I couldn't find my glasses. I tore the entire house apart looking for them. The more I looked, the more aggravated I became, throwing items around and stalking around the house like a madman. I noticed that Gina was sitting in the living room chair shaking her head with a smirk on her face. Finally, I said, "Why don't you help me look instead of just sitting there?"

She asked, "You want me to help?"

Miraculously controlling my temper, I said, "Yes! If you don't mind!"

"Okay," she said. "I'll help. Why don't you check your face?"

Of course, I had been wearing them the whole time! I couldn't believe it. At that instant, I found myself in the middle of two conflicting emotions. I could feel my bad mood escalating. A part of me was angry at Gina for letting me search the entire house when she knew we were going to be late for the dinner. This could have easily turned into an argument that would have set the tone for the rest of the evening. But something inside me knew what the consequences would be if I held on to the anger. So when I looked at Gina, who was trying with all her might to refrain from laughing, I decided to go with the positive emotion and began to laugh too. I looked at Gina and said, "Oh yeah. Right where I left them. You're never going to let me live this one down, are you?"

As we were leaving, Gina noticed I was jiggling the keys in my hand. "Now," she said, "if you can only find your car keys we might make it in time for dessert!"

We laughed all the way to the restaurant as we recalled some of the more ridiculous things I had done in the past. Laughter put us both in a relaxed, positive mood, which set the tone for an enjoyable and very successful evening.

It is amazing the power we derive when we step outside our emotions of the moment, give ourselves permission to make a shift, and view them from a humorous perspective. Remember, your Humor Being is a part of your higher self. It's the part of you that brings out the best in you when times get tough. But you don't have to be a comedian, with an arsenal of rapid-fire funny remarks or wisecracks at your disposal, to give your Humor Being the opportunity to express itself. What's important is not necessarily to *be* funny, but rather to allow yourself to *see* the funny in a stressful or challenging situation. This is a habit that anyone can master. The more you challenge yourself to see the humor during adverse times, the more your Humor Being will become a part of who you are. The more your Humor Being becomes a part of who you are, the more you will be able to enjoy your life.

So, when do you need to tap into your Humor Being? When you become aware that your emotions are veering out of control. How do you determine they're heading in that direction? Stop, take a deep breath, and ask yourself any number of the following warning questions:

"What will be the consequences if I hold on to this anger?"

"I have an important meeting with a client. Am I putting my best foot forward now?"

"What will happen if I don't get my shift together?"

"I have an extremely busy day. Am I in the mood I need to be in to get things done?"

"Are my fears keeping me from succeeding?"

"What can I do to turn this mood around?"

"What would Steve Rizzo say if he could see me now?" (Or substitute "my mother" for "Steve Rizzo" and "she" for "he.")

These types of questions act like radar, warning you that you're spinning out of control and becoming dangerously negative. More important, warning questions are good reminders that there are better ways to deal with frustrating and chaotic events than clinging to the worst-case scenarios that they bring up.

Here is one humorous strategy to get you on your way. The next time you're at the point of losing it, imagine that your Humor Being has a voice and is taking on the role of a news reporter giving you the blow-by-blow account of what is happening inside you.

"We interrupt your regularly scheduled life to bring you this special news bulletin! This is a message from your emotional broadcasting system. It has been brought to our attention that you are late, stuck in traffic, and your back sweat is turning your seat into the Everglades! You are now being tested to evaluate the severity of the negative situation. Right now you have a choice! You can either get your shift together and laugh, learn the lesson life is trying to teach you, nourish your soul, move on with confidence, and enjoy the day, or you can suffer from inner conflict, get angry, lose control, and let opportunities pass you by! May the shift be with you. Back to you in the studio, Chuck."

A Super Humor Being

Sometimes it takes a great amount of courage to learn the lessons that life puts in front of us that enable us to grow. Many things of value cannot be taught; they must be lived. Every now and then, however, people come into our lives and set the ultimate example for what it means to be courageous and take responsibility. Once in a while we are blessed to know those who set the standard for what it means to be a hero, simply by the choices they make. One such person was Christopher Reeve.

I mentioned Christopher Reeve earlier in the book, but the following story warrants mention. On May 3, 2004, just five months before he passed away, I had the pleasure of meeting and talking with Chris and Dana Reeve. Chris and I were both speaking in front of a group of 5,000 Choice Hotel employees at the San Diego Convention Center. We "bookended" the event as opening and closing keynote speakers.

After my speech, I was approached by Dana. She greeted me with a hug, congratulated me on the favorable reception I had received, and asked me to come back to meet Chris. She told me that when I gave my speech, she and Chris were watching my performance on a TV in the green room. Dana beamed as she told me that there were eight other people in the room with them and Chris told them all to keep quiet or please leave because he wanted to hear the end of my presentation.

"Needless to say," she said anyway, "there was silence."

I guess when Superman speaks, people listen.

When I made it back to where Chris was waiting, he smiled and thanked me for coming back to say hello. He said that he really appreciated what I had to say, especially the part about unleashing the power of your Humor Being. "I live by that philosophy," he said. That was the best compliment I ever received in my speaking career. Hearing it from Chris Reeve humbled me but also reinforced that what I'd been talking about all these years could actually make a difference in people's lives.

When Reeve and I spoke he shared his philosophy of life. "Please don't accept absolutes. Don't become paralyzed literally and figuratively by what other people say you can or can't do. Don't let anyone set your limits. Set your own goals and have the discipline to obtain them. If you fall short, deal with it later. Reach as high as you can."

Setting an example of this magnificent attitude was not only a triumph for Christopher Reeve and those with spinal cord injuries, but speaks of the power of the human spirit. Carol Ryff, professor of psychology at the University of Wisconsin–Madison, says this about Reeve: "There is no doubt in my mind his positive attitude extended his life, probably dramatically. The fact that it didn't allow him to recover function of all limbs is beside the point. There is a science that is emerging that says a positive attitude isn't just a state of mind. It is also connected to what is going on in the brain and in the body."

There is also scientific research emerging about the enigmatic healing power of humor and the effect it has on the brain and in the body. I believe a sense of humor and a positive attitude are inextricably linked. After all, it's rare that you walk away from a deep, genuine laugh or even a smile and fail to feel more positive than you did before.

As Christopher Reeve told me and I later read in his book, it was partly through humor that he came to understand that his fear-based thoughts didn't have to affect his reality. In the chapter entitled "Humor" from his book *Nothing Is Impossible*, Reeve recounts the interaction between him and his nurse that let him know he was on the road to recovery.

Nurse: "How are you today?"

Reeve: "Well, my throat is a little scratchy, I have an itch on my nose, and my fingernails need cutting. Oh, and I'm paralyzed."

Jokes about the wheelchair helped to defuse his anger about being in one. Knowing that Jay Leno is an avid car collector, Reeve made an offer to the host of *The Tonight Show*:

"When I am out of this chair you can have it. Put a Chevy 350 engine in it, and blast down the freeway!"

When David Letterman asked him how he was doing, Christopher told him, "I'm fine, but I think I broke my neck again driving over the potholes on my way into the city."

This type of humor helped him to adjust to his new way of living. In fact, humor was one of the things that brought some kind of normalcy and balance into his life.

"How nice it is to be teased," said Reeve. "I love it when I approach the dinner table, which I occasionally hit as I try to park, and my son picks up his plate and says, 'Look out for the crazy driver!'"

While trying to adjust to his new life, Reeve would often slip into what he called "the numb zone." The numb zone, according to Reeve, is a very dangerous place to be: a gray area that is devoid of human emotion and life energy. It's when you're completely unengaged—not depressed, but not able to generate enthusiasm either. That's when turning to humor can become difficult, but all the more necessary.

"Sometimes humor is hard," Christopher said, acknowledging the difficulty in laughing when you don't feel like it. "But it's worth it."

I agree: humor is worth it because it gives you the motivation and attitude to move forward. Humor shrinks negative thoughts before they blossom into full-blown emotional havoc. Had Christopher Reeve held on to the thoughts that were telling him what he couldn't be, what he'd never be again, he would most certainly have been paralyzed mentally, emotionally, and spiritually. He would have lived—and we would have witnessed—a totally different outcome to his situation.

When Chris was asked how he kept it together, his reply was, "Mostly with duct tape. It keeps the hose from falling off the ventilation that keeps me alive." It was often his quick wit that allowed him to avoid falling prey to the devastating consequences of negative thinking. His innate ability to make the shift and laugh in the face of fear gave this Superman, this Super-Humor-Being, the courage to carry on and accomplish so much in the last nine years of his life. It is this same attitude we all need if we are to succeed and enjoy our lives, regardless of our personal circumstances.

It is my observation, however, that our culture is becoming ever so serious and politically correct. I fear some of you out there may be in the final stages of stifling your humor genes, thus running the risk of forgetting the benefits of laughter altogether. Why not laugh in the midst of a major challenge at work? Why not find some levity during extreme difficulty?

When I give my workshop I explain to my audience that one way to tap into their laughter reserve is to turn on the TV and challenge themselves to view the news as if it were Comedy Central. Here's an example of something I heard on the news: 1 percent of this planet's ozone layer is gone. That's pretty serious stuff, right? But do you know what the main reason for this is? Cow gas. That's right, cow gas. I'm not kidding. Studies have shown that the methane from cow gas is actually destroying the ozone. Apparently they found this out by weighing it. I started thinking, "Weighing it? How do you weigh cow gas? And who's the guy that has this job? And what's his job title? Bovine flatulence engineer?" All of a sudden your job doesn't seem that bad after all, does it? You have to think that everybody makes fun of this guy. Even the cows must make fun of this guy.

Cow number 1: "Hey, he's right in back of you."

Cow number 2: "I know. I just ripped one so hard, milk came out of my nose!"

Cow number 1: "What's he doing now?"

Cow number 2: "He's crying, that's what he's doing!"

Cow number 1: "Hey, Elsie, do me a favor. Pull my hoof!"

Here's an irony. When something upsetting happens, we often find ourselves retreating into a darkened room to pray for guidance, thus neglecting laughter as an ally to help us heal. I'm not suggesting that we shouldn't pray, but I can't stress enough the importance of taking time out to laugh throughout the course of a day, especially when times are tough.

ATTITUDE ADJUSTMENT STRATEGY:
Unleash the power of your Humor Being every day.

Unleash your humorous side every day, and I mean *every* day. Your Humor Being is of your higher self. It's the part of you that brings out the best in you when times get tough. What your Humor Being can give you more than anything else is emotional stability. I think that about says it all.

What It Means to Be Positive

9

In the middle of difficulty
lies opportunity.

ALBERT EINSTEIN

nyone can tell you that one key to living a happy, successful life is having a positive attitude, especially during adverse times. I know that sometimes it's impossible to justify the depth of misfortune we encounter. I know that sometimes it seems impossible to stand tall and be positive when it feels like your world is crashing down. But I also know that we all have what it takes to deal with misfortune when it occurs. It may be easier said than done, but this is what acquiring a positive attitude is all about. It's about fortifying yourself for a fight with a very real enemy: your own negativity.

I tend to think of life as a battlefield—albeit a metaphorical one, very different from the physical and mental horrors of war that my own brother experienced. Can anyone deny that bloodless battles rage around us every day, often fought against familiar enemies that loom from the past? The cause of these everyday battle wounds vary: a bitter divorce, the loss of a loved one, financial problems, unemployment, health issues, and the list goes on and on. However, one thing is certain: these emotional casualties sustained on the battlefield of everyday life can be as devastating to your long-term well-being as missing 21 feet of small intestine.

It's easy to become overwhelmed and crushed by a negative situation, and to give up before you give yourself a significant chance to rebound. It's at these times you are at your most vulnerable; your emotional warning system is at red alert and you can easily enter the Negative Zone where it seems like the entire world is against you. That's when the launching of fearful, destructive thoughts begins, like a salvo of rockets aimed at nothing in particular. It's at these times especially that you must be hyper-aware of both your mental and verbal output.

The shrapnel of those explosive thoughts and words inflicts emotional wounds that cause you to believe that you are being victimized and cheated.

This is a situation in which a "foxhole mentality" can be of value. If it comes down to you (and your inner thoughts) against the world, wouldn't you want a companion that isn't willing to make a quick surrender?

"My life isn't working." (Boom!)

"I'll never live my dream." (Bang!)

"I'll never find someone who will love me for who I am." (Incoming!)

"I don't have what it takes to handle this." (It was really an honor to serve alongside myself.)

"My life is one big mess." (We are sorry to inform you that your confidence is dead. There was nothing we could do.)

This constant bombardment of fearful negative thoughts and words explode with tremendous force in your subconscious and cause you to see (and further create) a reality that you believe to be true. The result: you have lost the battle. You have let your defenses down and your life has been taken over by your own rogue thoughts and words and you are vulnerable to hopelessness.

Hopelessness is dangerous, because when you concede all hope, you actually seal your fate and finalize your destiny. If you find yourself stuck in hopelessness, lock your car doors and call someone you trust to come give you a jump, ASAP. Without hope, there is no room to even consider other options, let alone a miracle. (And all hockey fans know that miracles can happen.)

I'm not passing judgment on anyone who allows dark moments to go by. There are valid reasons for bad feelings to occur during difficult times, and it takes an incredible amount of fortitude to give thanks for the good things when so much is lost. However, if you expect to prevail during tough times you must understand that it is your current perception of the situation that either gives you hope or makes you want to give up to a lost cause. If you're always thinking about how badly life is treating you, if you are always telling stories about how you can't get a fair shake, you will always feel miserable. Ever hear the old saying, "Misery loves company"? Being miserable doesn't exactly attract good things, does it? If you want to change your life for the better, start by consciously changing what you think and what you say.

Speak Words That Empower You

I have often been asked, "What was the most valuable lesson you learned from your brother?" Without hesitation, my response is always, "Never use your words to describe a challenging situation. Rather, use your words to change your perspective on a challenging situation. And by the way, if you want spaghetti and meatballs or a hero sandwich, don't let anyone tell you that you can't have it."

It's true that what you think is what you get, but what you say out loud in the midst of troubling times has even greater impact. Although it may be possible to convince yourself that you're trying to stay positive when the situation calls for some good old-fashioned angst, what you say out loud during those times could very well make the difference in how long you remain in that situation and how deeply you are affected. The words you speak amplify your feelings and trigger mental images. If what you think is what you get, then what you say is what you ask for.

The best defense for any kind of negative assault on our emotions is to go on the offensive against that nasty voice that has been hardwired into our heads. No matter how big the problem, no matter how intense your troubles, no matter how overwhelming a situation may seem, it's always fear-based thoughts and defensive emotions, as well as beliefs that have been built from past experiences and from the negative words we use, that result in the loss of control of our emotions. When we lose control of our emotions, pretty quickly thereafter we lose control of the situation we find ourselves in.

The best way to take control is to stop worrying and complaining about your plight and start talking back to the negative voice in your head. Talk back to that voice that's articulating the defeatist language invading your brain and is taking a direct verbal pass out into the world:

"Here we go again."

"Why is this happening to me?"

"Why can't I ever get a break?"

"I will never be able to handle this."

"I never get a break."

"I'm not lucky."

"Good things never happen to me."

"What's the use? No one cares anyway."

These words are not only self-defeating in the moment, but keep you from seeing possibilities to a brighter outcome or finding solutions to problems.

Awareness is the first step in stifling this voice and turning a compulsively negative mindset around. Once you recognize the dismal reality these thoughts and words help you create for yourself, you can step back, observe the direction you are going in, and take action against them. You do this by counterattacking with empowering thoughts and words that instill hope, faith, confidence, courage, and determination.

Whatever it is that is bringing you down, acknowledge the fear it represents and immediately go on the offensive and bombard those fears with emotionally charged words. And if you're worried about someone catching you talking to yourself and thinking you're crazy, just hop in the car or take a walk and give that voice in your head a piece of your mind.

"Hey, I know you're there and I know what you're trying to do. But it won't work! Because I'm in control here! I get to choose what thoughts flow through my mind! I get to choose the words that are coming out of my mouth! But most of all, I have a force (God, or whatever you choose to believe) that is bigger than anything you can throw at me! So go ahead! Hit me with your best shot! One thing is certain: I will prevail! I've got my shift together!"

Do you see how empowering, emotionally charged words like these can lift your spirits and propel you to move forward? Whether coming from a positive or negative place, your words inevitably affect your attitude, and thus your situation. The moment you open your mouth to say something, you start the process of creating a new, more positive reality and outcome.

Doesn't it make sense that the more positive your thoughts and words are, the more confident you will feel? The easier it will be to shift perspective and see the alternative actions that are open to you?

That's what gives you hope and enables you to see a higher outcome. And that's how you acquire a positive attitude.

When adversity strikes, your perception of yourself and the world around you are key factors to ensure your well-being. If the words you speak aloud reflect weakness, inadequacy, or victimization, then the energy you send out will mirror those same qualities.

On the other hand, if the words you speak reflect courage, power, and a view of life as a never-ending adventure and learning experience, then the energy you send out will mirror those words, filling you with hope and a sense of the opportunities ahead, thus enabling you to win the day-to-day battles that lead to a fulfilling life.

When life gets hard and things don't go as planned, it is what you say out loud that will cause you to either resent it or surrender to it. The surrender I'm referring to involves letting go and yielding to something greater. It's an inner awareness that allows you to step back and see the bigger picture—that how you view these events and the actions you take are more important than the actual events themselves. As I've said before, my brother is a perfect example of this philosophy. Gradually he was able to let go and allow himself to embrace the changes that were taking place in his life. By doing so, he was able to give himself a fighting chance to create a positive experience full of previously unconsidered (and therefore unexpected) opportunities.

At this juncture, I want to address the word *positive* and the frustration that can arise from its use. Oftentimes I will get pushback from people when I suggest that they approach their problems from a positive point of view. "How can you expect me to be positive when nothing in my life is working?" Or, "It's easy for you to feel blessed, you didn't lose someone you love." Or, "If I hadn't lost my job, I could feel positive too."

Perhaps a different interpretation of what it means to be positive is called for; that is, being positive isn't a Disney movie, it's not being in control of our emotions, is not always being perfect nor about feeling good all the time. True positivity is knowing that we learn from our mistakes, and it allows us to move forward with optimism. Being positive causes us to understand that learning from our mistakes helps us become better people: richer, deeper, and more resilient.

Being positive doesn't mean that we are always smiling and enjoying every moment of our lives. Give me a break! It's knowing that sometimes it's okay to cry, mourn, and feel sad, that it's okay to get angry and lose our temper. Hey, it's healthy to feel bad sometimes. It means you're not a robot. So don't worry, okay? Your positivity license won't be revoked.

People who are generally positive have problems just like everyone else. What separates the chronically positive from everyone else is that they know that their problems won't last and are simply part of the process of life. Positive people are the ultimate shift-heads. They always find ways to shift their perspective and hold on to the things that bring them joy. This is a quality that keeps them from feeling victimized. Pain is unavoidable, but to a person with a positive attitude, that's all it is: pain. It is not something to be compounded by doubt and past experience.

Positive people instinctively know that adversity is necessary in order to grow. We are here on earth to experience, learn, grow, and become the person we are meant to be. How we choose to experience what happens to us, be it good or bad, will dictate our life lessons. What we learn determines how we grow, and this continued growth is what shapes who and what we become. If we can truly comprehend this, it will help free us from feeling victimized when times are tough. Viewing life through a positive filter will allow us to fulfill our potential and just maybe help us to compare a challenging situation to a pop quiz in Life 101, rather than, say, the apocalypse. In short, positive people really have their shift together!

Seeing the Good in Adversity

On August 10, 2003, I was sitting in the intensive care waiting room at Good Samaritan Hospital on Long Island. My mother was unconscious and in critical condition, the result of a lifetime of ailments and complications. Doctors had told us she could remain that way for days or even weeks before passing on.

I was faced with a difficult decision. On August 12, I needed to be in Chicago to finish editing my PBS special *Becoming a Humor Being*. Time was of the essence. I needed to have the project completed in time for it to be aired in the fall schedule. I had many gut-wrenching heart-to-hearts with my family, and they all assured me that the right thing to do would be for me to go to Chicago for two days, complete the editing, and come back. If there were any changes in my mother's condition, they promised to notify me. In an effort to make my decision a little easier, everyone assured me that it was what Mom would have wanted.

As I sat in one of the institutional plastic waiting room chairs remembering some of the experiences my mother and I had shared, the pay phone in the waiting room began to ring. An orderly answered and called out that there was a phone call for "a Steve Rizzo." I was surprised, to say the least, wondering who would call me at a pay phone at the hospital. I picked up the phone, and the voice on the other end said, "Steve, I love you. I'm thinking about you, and if you want me there with you, I will catch the next plane to New York." It was my dear friend Jeffrey Gitomer. I asked how he knew about my mom and how he got the number to the pay phone in my exact location. He simply said, "Sometimes friends have a way of knowing."

When I hung up the phone, a feeling of appreciation washed over me. I knew Jeff would have been on the next plane if I had told him I needed him. I felt truly blessed to have such wonderful friends who were there for me in my time of need. I was also grateful for my family's willingness to put their pain aside to take on the task of helping to ease my mind. They not only showed tremendous empathy, but helped me make a tough decision at a very difficult time. Recognizing these simple blessings was a huge step in helping me to stay positive in that moment and enabled me to take care of my professional responsibilities.

At around 2 a.m. on August 12, I was sleeping in my Chicago hotel room when the phone rang. It was my wife, Gina, informing me that my mother had passed. She stressed that there was no need for me to return home right away. After all, the wake services wouldn't begin for another two days. The family consensus was that I should complete my project and then return to New York.

When I hung up the phone, I was overcome with two separate emotions: grief for the loss of my mother and guilt for not being by her side. I packed my bags and lay down to try and sleep. I didn't know whether I was going to stay or go and wondered how I was going to muster enough courage to get through the coming days. I prayed for strength and guidance to do the right thing.

Later that morning, I was sitting in the editing room at WTTW Studios in Chicago with Jack, the director of the special; Frank and Paul, the editors; and Kim, director of production services. I must have been unusually quiet, because Kim asked me if I was okay. I told everyone that my mom had passed away the night before. There was a slight pause, and Jack asked, "Why are you here?"

"I don't know," I said. "I think I'm supposed to be here. I think it's what she would want. I'll be home in time for the wake services." There was a long awkward pause as I said a silent prayer for the strength to get through the day and stared at my shoes, feeling like a jackass.

The phone rang and Paul picked it up. "Steve," he said, "it's for you. It's a Nido Qubein."

A little flummoxed, I said, "What's going on here? First I get a phone call at a pay phone in a waiting room in a hospital, and now I get a call in an editing room in Chicago. I feel like I'm in *The Matrix*. How do these people know where I am?"

Nido was a relatively new friend, someone I had met several years before through the National Speakers Association. He is one of those people who radiate such positive energy that you can actually feel it, even in a long-distance phone call. The conversation was short, but his voice was calm and soothing. His tone was sincere. He let me know how much he cared and that he understood the difficulty of my situation. His parting words were, "Sometimes we have to do what we have to do, even when we're feeling pain."

Nido had no way of knowing the impact of that short conversation, but he was the answer to my prayer for strength and guidance. At that moment, I just knew I was supposed to be where I was.

I hung up the phone and took a deep breath. I could feel my emotions getting the best of me. I had been thinking about it and decided to let everyone know that I was dedicating the TV show to the memory of Jacqueline Rizzo, my mother. As soon as I made my announcement, the tears began to flow. I knew there was no holding back, so I didn't try to fight it. I wasn't embarrassed and I didn't make a move to leave the room. I just sat there with my hands over my eyes and cried. It was as if a dam had burst open after years of intense pressure. Then something unexpected happened. Jack got up from his chair and stood behind me with his hands on my shoulders. Kim sat down next to me and took my right hand in hers. Paul and Frank turned around in their chairs to silently watch the tableau. We all had tears in our eyes. No words were spoken, but my grief and their sympathy were palpable. There was a total understanding and acceptance. I know they were feeling my pain, and yet, at the same time, they were healing my pain.

Sensing the need for some comic relief, I managed to blubber, "Why is everyone crying? Did your mothers pass away last night too?" Everyone started laughing. Then, in that instant, all ten of the TV monitors in the room began flashing the title of my PBS special, *Becoming a Humor Being.*

"That's strange," Paul said. "Nobody touched anything. That's not the kind of thing that just happens by itself."

Laughing and staring at the flashing monitors, I said, "They didn't go on by themselves! That's my mom telling me I should be here. Let's get to work!"

I will always remember that moment as something utterly special. Although I was consumed by pain, I could still see and feel the goodness in my life. The phone calls from friends, the support of my family, and the bonding with people I hardly knew renewed my faith in the power of the human spirit. It reinforced my belief that we all share a connection and reminded me that life goes on after all. It's truly miraculous when we can allow ourselves to feel so grateful for what we have, even when we've lost so much.

Life is full of disappointment and heartache; good and bad experiences are simply part of the process of life. In fact, they provide a point of comparison. It's necessary to feel the effect of one to appreciate the other. Life would indeed be boring and unfulfilling without the highs and lows that naturally occur. This is the wonder and, yes, the blessing of being alive. So in the big picture of life, even when bad things happen, if we can look at that bad thing from a more neutral position, then we will truly understand that there is no bad experience, only a bad attitude.

With practice, we can learn to have a positive attitude during tough times. When adversity strikes, positive thoughts are not naturally what spring to mind. Negative thoughts attack and at times bombard us with a vengeance. But if you are on guard and use the power of choice to work for you, you will come to understand that circumstances, no matter how severe, do not have to determine your fate. Rather, it's what you choose to do about your circumstances and who you choose to become that matters.

Life is an ongoing obstacle course, always challenging you to be the best you can be. Each obstacle, no matter how big or small, is an opportunity for you to make the choice to shift your perspective and view it through the eyes of hope and peace. As I said earlier, this is what acquiring a positive attitude is all about. This is what builds your character and enables you to grow. This is also why some of your biggest challenges can be blessings in disguise. When shift happens, your life changes. Understanding this is the pathway to success and happiness.

Positive people do not get a free pass from life's pain. They simply have ways of feeling the pain, recognizing that the situation calls for a new viewpoint, and shifting their perspective. When the tears are gone they choose to seek the joy that the world still has to offer. In short, positive people really have their shift together.

A Power Shift in Focus

The most important lesson that I've learned from living on this planet is what any truly happy, successful, and optimistic person knows about life: that they will experience good times and bad times; that they will have sad days and ecstatic moments; that nothing in life is permanent and our success and happiness depend on our ability to ride these waves of change with equanimity.

Happy, successful, optimistic people are not exempt from the trials and tribulations of life. In fact, some of the happiest, most successful, and most optimistic people I know have had to overcome unbelievably difficult circumstances to get to where they are today.

But what they all have in common is their uncanny ability to shift their focus to a higher part of themselves. They allow themselves to temporarily step away from those moments that are bringing them down or are causing them pain and immediately begin to focus on aspects of their lives that bring them joy and lift their spirits. They feel blessed for the things that life has given them rather than cursing what life has denied them or the unwanted things life is throwing at them. I admire the way they find the laughter during tough times and sometimes even during the worst of times. It is not a question of putting blinders on and ignoring that they are going through a difficult time, but rather that they instinctively know when to shift their mindset to something that will put them on a more productive path. In reality, we all have the power to do this. It's what I call a Power Shift in Focus.

Being able to create a Power Shift in Focus is one habit that can have a tremendous impact on your life. Why? Because it's a direct answer to the question life is always asking of you: "Who do you think you are?" When you temporarily step away from challenging situations and steer your attention to something that makes you feel good, you are thereby replenishing your spirit and nourishing your soul, the very essence of who you are. You are recharging your inner battery with the emotional fortitude needed to forge ahead. When you do go back to face the situation that is causing unease in your life, which inevitably you must do, you will feel less overwhelmed and the answers will come to you more readily. This is because you've calmed your nervous system down to the point where you can embrace the situation rather than have it control you.

You can't stop life from throwing stuff at you. You can't stop the unexpected from interfering with your goals and dreams. But you can choose how to respond. You can always choose to shift to a positive state of mind when unwanted things happen. People who are happy, successful, and optimistic know that no matter what happens, life still goes on and they can choose to focus on things that empower them. They refuse to give up their right to enjoy life. And guess what. So can you.

My friend Kelly, a warm, energetic, and incredibly sympathetic person, is a good example of what a Power Shift in Focus is all about. In a conversation I had with Kelly shortly after her mother passed away, she told me that although it was very emotionally distressing to witness her mom's protracted battle with cancer, it also made her realize the blessings in her life.

Bearing witness to a loved one's death is of course one of the most painful experiences we can have. Kelly confessed that her anxiety over the illness was affecting her relationships with her family and hampering her enthusiasm at work. She found it difficult to enjoy her life. Something had to change or she feared that the profound effects of the illness would overtake her and lead her into a full-blown depression. The choices that Kelly made to rectify her situation were indeed life-changing, but the realization that she had the power to make those choices was actually quite simple.

One day before entering the hospital to visit her mother, Kelly noticed that her personal attitude was different. She felt a sense of confidence and acceptance about her mother's condition and felt strangely at peace. She thought back over her trip to the hospital, thinking that everything was as usual: same route, same time, and same daily routine. But something was different. What was it? she wondered. Then Kelly realized that she had not been thinking of her mom during the drive to the hospital. Something funny her own children had done was commanding her attention, and she had been totally absorbed in that and the joy they brought her.

At that moment, Kelly had an intense understanding that although she was hurting, she could also simultaneously appreciate and enjoy her life. She realized it was unrealistic to deny herself the opportunity to feel the range of emotions that her mother's condition called from her, and she gave herself permission to freely express her grief. There were times when it felt as if the tears would never stop. After the tears, however, Kelly also gave herself permission to refocus her attention on aspects of her life that made her feel good. She vowed to herself that throughout the course of each day she would stop and make conscious choices to focus on the many wonderful things for which she was grateful.

For example, after an emotional visit at the hospital, Kelly would allow herself to feel the sadness that was associated with her mother's illness. But after she let go, cried, and cursed, she would shift her focus to her children and her husband. In fact, she even brought along pictures of them on her next visits, which helped her to remember the good times they had all had together. This prompted a sense of assurance that there would be many more good times to come. Kelly's newfound ability to refocus was empowering. It brought about an instant, overwhelming attitude of gratitude for her life, even though she was experiencing incredible sadness. Then Kelly decided to take the process a step further. On her drives to and from the hospital, she allowed herself to enjoy the view of the majestic homes, ever-changing landscape, and colorful scenery that rolled along outside her windows. This acknowledgment of the world around her pleased and calmed her, lifted her spirits, and helped her to appreciate how much life had to offer, even when she was hurting.

Kelly also found that when she gave herself permission to smile and appreciate her life, she was able to recapture the zest for life that she had once felt was at risk. And she found relief in the fact that she could still laugh out loud without feeling guilty. These new attitudes and coping strategies gave her the strength she needed to survive this tragic situation.

A Power Shift in Focus, even if only for a very few moments, can have a profound effect on how you cope with any challenge and help you understand the great duality of life. In other words, you can't know true peace until you've experienced chaos. You can't know joy unless you've felt pain. Conversely, no matter how many tears may fall, there is still room for a smile, and even laughter. You must experience one end of the emotional spectrum to fully appreciate the other. A Power Shift in Focus is a skill that nourishes your soul and significantly changes how you view life. It can be improved with practice and is a key to creating a happy life for yourself.

> ### ATTITUDE ADJUSTMENT STRATEGY:
> #### Practice a Power Shift in Focus.
>
> Temporarily step away from those moments that are bringing you down and focus on aspects of yourself that lift you up. Bless the things that life has given you, rather than cursing what you are lacking. And always find the laughter during tough times. This is what happy, successful, and optimistic people know.

High Points to Remember

- When something upsetting happens, it's your thoughts about the situation that will either minimize or magnify its effect.

- When you shift your thoughts, you change the way you feel, and when you change the way you feel, you change your life experience.

- Being positive doesn't mean that you should always smile and enjoy life; it's knowing that sometimes it's okay to cry, mourn, and feel sad. You don't always have to be in control of your emotions. It's okay to sometimes get angry and lose your temper. Don't worry. Your positive license won't get revoked.

- Your Humor Being is of your higher self. It's the part of you that brings out the best in you when times get tough.

- A Power Shift in Focus can change how you view life and significantly help you to solve problems.

Part 4

The Shift Continues

Faith is the antidote to despair and laughter is the music of faith.

DEAN KOONTZ

In this section I will show you how awareness, common sense, and your sense of humor can change your perception on two imposing forces: fear and the Big Mouth inside your head.

Fear is the emotion from which anger, worry, guilt, self-doubt, and all other negative emotions derive. I call all negative emotions the Destroyers of the Spirit. The Big Mouth inside your head is that inner voice I referred to earlier that plays off your deep-rooted fears and keeps you in a constant state of turmoil.

The moment you become aware of the deceiving ways of the Big Mouth and allow yourself to laugh in the face of fear, you enter into a higher state of consciousness.

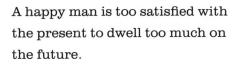

The Big Mouth Inside Your Head

10

A happy man is too satisfied with the present to dwell too much on the future.

ALBERT EINSTEIN

As we've already discussed, the present is the only place where your life can happen. Not the past, not the future. The present is also the only place where happiness and peace can be experienced. Sadly, though, the past and future are where many people choose to live their lives. Failure to understand that "now" is the only moment in which life is actually taking place is a major cause of unhappiness. Equally important to understand is that whatever happens in the now, there is always a choice in how to respond. How you respond will be the ultimate deciding factor in the quality of peace and happiness you will have.

When negative emotions are getting the best of me and I'm having difficulty being happy and at peace in the moment, it's primarily due to one of four reasons:

The first is when I'm in a situation that isn't going the way I think it should: being stuck in traffic, worrying about the weather, people aren't cooperating, dealing with disappointing outcomes, and so on. When I'm in this state I'm actually allowing circumstances that are beyond my control to hijack my emotions and rob me of peace in the moment.

The second is when I'm feeling doubt that I will ever receive something that I feel entitled to. This could be any number of things: a promotion, more money, power, or fame. When I'm in this state, I'm putting my happiness on hold until what I believe I deserve comes into my life. The harsh reality here is that the more negative feelings I harbor, the more difficult it will be for me to achieve and/ or receive the things I want.

The third is when I'm anxious about something in the near future: the uncertainty of a challenging day ahead, financial security, concerns about family, or even achieving a distant goal. When I'm in this state I'm surrendering my happiness and peace of mind in the moment because I'm worrying about something I think might or might not happen in the future. If I continue to obsess about the future with fear and worry, I could very well create a self-fulfilling prophecy. In other words, the very things I'm worried about could actually come to pass. Remember, thoughts are the first steps in the creation of our future, and if you think it enough, it becomes your reality.

The fourth is when something happened to me in the past that is causing me to feel some kind of negativity in the present: guilt, fear, or anger. It could be something I did or failed to do or someone else did or failed to do. Either way, it's causing me to feel unease in the present. I actually believe that if that something had not happened the way it did, I would be at peace and happy in the now. When I'm in this state (and this one makes me laugh when I think about it), I'm actually convincing myself that even though something happened to me 24 hours ago, or 15 years ago, I deserve to let it keep me from being successful and enjoying my life. I guess I'll show me a thing or two!

This all sounds crazy, doesn't it? Well, all aboard the Crazy Train, folks—that is, if you can find room, because we all fall victim to this type of madness in one way or another.

Fortunately, I've become aware of the culprit that keeps me from living in and enjoying the current moment. I call it The Big Mouth inside my head. And guess what? We all have one. You can call it whatever you like. Many people call this Big Mouth inside their head the ego. Some call it the enemy. Some even call it the devil, which might be appropriate, albeit a little melodramatic, because if you listen to it there will be hell to pay. I call it the Big Mouth for one obvious reason: it never shuts up.

This voice inside your head may be barely noticeable, but believe me, it can be overpowering. Or it can be unbearably loud—so loud, in fact, that even though you're trying to tune it out, you can't help but be affected by it. It is expressed as that uneasy feeling you have that tells you the only way that you can be happy is if something specific happens, if you become this or achieve that. It's the voice that plays off of your deep-rooted fears. "What if I don't have enough money?" "What if I fail?" "I'll probably get sick!" "I knew this would happen!" "I'll never have an intimate, meaningful relationship!"

All of these worries are fear-based beliefs you bring from your past. That's what the Big Mouth does: it empowers demons from your past to poison and bedevil the moment. The Big Mouth (oh, that sly little devil) cunningly keeps those toxic beliefs from your past alive in your mind. It forces you to remember the hurt and disappointment from days or years gone by, so that when the opportunity for you to succeed or enjoy the moment presents itself, those destructive memories attack like emotional piranhas, devouring any chance you have for happiness.

The Big Mouth's main mission is to keep your toxic labels alive. It's a great deceiver and creates stories that will convince you that you cannot achieve success and enjoy the moment. This voice that never shuts up thrives on negative energy and operates from a lethal database in your mind that is filled with deep-rooted unconscious thoughts and beliefs that can distort your reality at will. It lives to twist the truth and spin lies that give you seemingly valid reasons to complain, blame, and tell your woe-is-me story to the world.

When the past impinges upon your present peace, crippling negative emotions like fear, anger, resentment, worthlessness, and worry consume your life. These Destroyers of the Spirit knock the life right out of you. You identify with them because they are accompanied by a swarm of negative thoughts and an involuntary compulsive way of thinking. Over a period of time, these thoughts lead you to believe that life is one big war zone and every day is an uphill battle. One hell of a way to live, isn't it? There is no way you can achieve happiness, much less peace, amid the white noise that accompanies these emotions.

It would be wonderful if I could say, "Well, just don't listen to the Big Mouth. Simply ignore it." I mean, you're pretty good at that, right? Just ask your wife, husband, or boss. Think of any one of your annoying relatives or in-laws and how you just tune them out when the noise becomes too negative. Go ahead, admit it, here, between us. When the bigmouthed people in your life become too negative, you can simply walk away.

Unfortunately, you don't have the same luxury with the Big Mouth in your head, because no matter where you go, your head is always with you. At least I hope it is. And as much as you may try, it's hard to completely ignore or tune out the constant ranting of the Big Mouth. So what happens? The Big Mouth creates emotional discord in your life that ruins your chance of real happiness.

Awareness Will Set You Free

The first step to freeing yourself from the Big Mouth inside your head is to be aware of it. You heard me right. Just be aware. Or as I sometimes like to say, "Awareness is the key that will set you free." Can I hear a "Hallelujah"? Sorry. I get a little carried away sometimes.

Breaking old beliefs and habits is dependent upon noticing them as the barriers to happiness that they are. Simply by being aware that you yourself are creating these barriers will open your mind to other possibilities. In other words, as soon as you notice that you are unhappy or not feeling right and recognize that the deceptive voice inside your head is responsible, you are able to shift to a higher place where you will be less likely to be affected. In this way you can begin to liberate yourself from identifying with the negativity that pervades your mind. One way to look at it is this: the Big Mouth leads you to your false self and awareness leads you to your higher self.

Symptoms of a Big Mouth in your head can include worrisome phrases like, "If only . . . ," "I should have . . . ," "I shouldn't have . . . ," "I can't . . . ," and thinking, "Holy crap, I sound like my mother/father!"

Here are some others:

"Nobody respects me."

"I never get a break."

"My parents never supported me."

"I swear I must be cursed."

"I was never loved."

"I will never have enough money!"

Guess what? The Big Mouth is at it again.

These are just a few indicators that the Mouth is yapping away. Other more intense symptoms include a fear of the present and future and a belief that you are not good enough, smart enough, or worthy enough to have what you want in life. These beliefs cause you to feel cheated or victimized and force you to lash out and blame, accuse, and complain. Catching these negative forces as soon after they are triggered is ideal. The longer they linger, the more damage they cause.

For a great part of my life I actually believed that it was safer and smarter not to take risks or chances. Every time the door of opportunity opened, the Big Mouth would do everything in its power to keep me from entering. "What, are you crazy? Remember what happened the last time you tried! Come on, you don't have what it takes! You better play it safe!"

As you can imagine, these habitual thoughts of imminent failure created major barriers in my life. What made these barriers even more difficult to penetrate was that they helped me rationalize why my life wasn't working. I believed that my plight was determined by my parents or authority figures and unfortunate circumstances beyond my control.

The bottom line is this: toxic labels ruin your life, and the Big Mouth inside your head gives those labels momentum. I'm going to share with you yet another episode from my life to illustrate exactly how toxic labels and the Big Mouth work together to instill fear and manipulate your life.

When I was in the eighth grade I was sitting with my parents in a guidance counselor's office. The purpose of the meeting was to map out my curriculum for my remaining years in high school, so that I would be prepared for the outside world once I graduated. I was nervous but very excited about fulfilling my dream of becoming a teacher. This guidance counselor didn't even know my name or what I was all about. He never asked me what my dreams or aspirations were. He didn't enter into any dialogue with me, nor did he say anything encouraging. He just looked at a folder and a stack of papers in it and proclaimed that I didn't have what it took to go to college. This proclamation became my death sentence, reinforcing what I already suspected was true—that I wasn't smart enough to succeed.

The real tragedy was that my parents and I put our faith and my future into the hands of someone who didn't know me. My parents were from the old school of thought. They were impressed by his title and considered him an expert in his field. He had to know what he was talking about. If he didn't, who did? We took his proclamation at face value and believed what he said about me.

To this day, I can still remember how I felt sitting in this man's office as he rambled on about my low test scores and other inadequacies. I was devastated, ashamed, and embarrassed. I couldn't bear to look at my parents. At the tender age of 14, I had the terrible feeling that I had let my parents down, that I wasn't smart enough to go to college and would never make them proud. Unfortunately, that moment became a defining aspect of my young life, and I truly began to wonder if I was smart enough to do anything at all.

I'm not saying that this one incident ruined my entire life. It was, however, one of many experiences that helped to confirm the already low opinion I had of myself. I'm well aware that some other student could have walked out of that guidance counselor's office and said, "I'll show him!" and used the entire incident as motivation to work harder and prove him wrong. Unfortunately, I was not that student and viewed the meeting through the eyes of my own toxic past.

I remember the empty feeling I had in high school as I sat as a spectator watching my brother play football and friends perform in school plays. Part of me thought I had the talent to participate, but the Big Mouth inside my head kept echoing these familiar words: "If you don't try, you can't fail."

I soon began to associate myself with the rebels of the school. They accepted me for who I was. Getting an education was not a priority. For the remainder of my school years I just went through the motions and barely managed to graduate.

When I entered the world of stand-up comedy my fear-based labels began to resurface with a vengeance. I guess on one level you could say I was very successful. After all, I was headlining comedy clubs throughout the country. I was pursuing and living a dream that many people envied. The problem was that I was living a lie. I wasn't the confident person I seemed to be, and I went on to conveniently ignore or sabotage the big opportunities that came my way. Let me explain.

Performing from club to club and being onstage wasn't the issue. In fact, comedy was my shield and my escape; I felt good about myself when I could make others laugh. I felt safe onstage and was at the top of my game. However, when it came to showing my talent to the industry big wheels (agents, casting directors, producers, etc.) I panicked and made excuses. I allowed my toxic label of being a failure and not good enough to determine my fate. Rather than planting my roots in the New York City or L.A. clubs, where comedy talent was discovered, I decided to hit the road as a headliner and play the circuit. Hence I allowed the Big Mouth to connive me into believing that it was safer to be a big fish in a small pond. Playing the circuit became a convenient excuse to avoid the industry. But what really knocks me out now, years later, is that I didn't understand that the reason I never got my "big break" was because of these very choices that I made.

When I finally began to investigate the causes of my unhappiness, I began to realize that my toxic labels and the Big Mouth inside my head were the primary culprits. Until then, I was unaware that my past experiences dictated so many of the choices I made in the present. The realization that these toxic labels and the Big Mouth were exerting so much unconscious power in my life became a real wake-up call. That awareness gradually helped to pull me away from my usual way of negative thinking. Every time I became aware, I simultaneously caught a glimpse of the real me and my own capability. This kind of constant awareness will eventually set you free. Why does awareness set you free? Because it's a higher state of consciousness that exists only in the present, where the Big Mouth, which draws its strength from fear-based beliefs from the past, has no real power.

The moment you say, "I'm not feeling right," or "There is definitely negative stuff going on inside of me that's controlling my life right now," you instantly shift into a state of awareness and clarity that allows you to expose this great adversary for what it really is: a distorted compilation of old destructive beliefs, mindsets, and thought patterns that promulgate false truths about yourself. The real freedom comes when you understand that you are not the Big Mouth (what a relief!) or the loser the Big Mouth is telling you that you are, but just a bystander who can step back and be aware of its presence and not take actions based on erroneous truths.

Common Sense and Humor

Being aware of the Big Mouth inside your head is the first step toward making your life all you want it to be, because awareness weakens the power of the Big Mouth and its influence over how you feel about yourself. Here's where your choices come in. Your next assignment, should you choose to accept it, is to nip those negative emotions in the bud before they blossom into emotional havoc. This may seem like a scene from *Mission: Impossible*, but have no fear, it is actually very doable. Once you take hold of your own emotional steering wheel, white knuckles or not, you can decide where you want to go.

Awareness provides the window of opportunity to challenge this big pain in the ass and liberate yourself from its toxicity! Now you can choose healthier, more productive ways of viewing situations that would otherwise impede your happiness and success, and you do so by employing step two, shifting into a mode of common sense or humor or both.

These steps are critical in warding off the assault on your self-esteem that's created by the constant bombardment of negative thinking and fear-based beliefs. The sooner you shift into either mode, the better. When worry, fear, anger, guilt, or any other negative emotion is given full rein, they gain momentum and incredible persuasive power.

But when you recognize that it is the Big Mouth who is pulling your strings and you challenge it with some good old-fashioned common sense and humor, you get that "Ah-ha" sensation, and at that moment a wonderful transformation begins to take place. The negative dialogue ceases, damaging emotions are weakened, and unhappiness starts to dissolve. Unhappiness cannot prevail if there is no unhappy dialogue to feed it.

Here's how step two works. Let's use the method of common sense first. As soon as you are aware of what the Big Mouth is up to, say, "I know who you are and I know what you're trying to do." Then, depending on the situation at hand, ask yourself some reasonable questions that allow you to tap into your own common sense, such as:

"What are the chances of this dreaded event happening?"

"Does it really help me to run through the same negative scenario and anxious thoughts over and over?"

"What is a more constructive way to view this situation?"

"What will the consequences be if I hold on to this fear, anger, guilt, or worry?"

These types of commonsense questions act as both a break and a buffer to help you to disassociate from further negativity, putting you in a more relaxed, reasonable state of mind.

Another way to stifle the Big Mouth and ward off negative assumptions from your past is to work with your Humor Being to rewrite your negative past experiences into a comedy with a happy ending. The whole point here is to use your imagination and have fun. That's exactly what I did years ago when I rewrote and redirected my eighth-grade counselor experience. Let me take you back in time.

The scene begins with me sitting with my mom and dad in the counselor's office, only this time there is one major difference. I have the ability to travel in time, which is exactly what I do. Before the meeting takes place I travel into the future and witness all of my accomplishments to date. When the counselor finally finishes mapping out my life he looks up at me and notices I'm smiling. "What in the world are you smiling at?" he asks. "This is serious stuff here. We're talking about your future!" I jump up and look at my mom and dad. Then I look right at the counselor. "No!" I say "*You* have been talking about my future! You've just spent the past half hour telling me what I will and will not be able to do with my life. You told me that I don't have what it takes to go to college. You gave me no hope. You never asked me about my dreams. And you haven't asked for my opinion, but I'm going to give it to you anyway!"

He looks at me as if he's going to say something, but I don't give him a chance. "First of all," I say, "I will go to college and I will graduate with honors. I will then go on to teach English to middle school students. I will then leave the school system and for 18 years I will headline comedy clubs all over the country. This will eventually lead me to star in many network and cable television shows. These experiences will be more than I ever dreamed possible. The people I meet will expand my capacity for love and compassion. The lessons I learn will be my reward for not listening to people like you!"

He jumps up from his seat to interrupt me, but I say, "Shut up and sit down. I'm not finished yet, bub!" (Remember, this is my script. I can rewrite and redirect it any way I want.) "After 18 years as a successful comedian I will make another major change. I will again follow my heart and enter the speaking forum and will create my own company, called Laugh It Off Productions. And I will use all of my life lessons to help people become happy and successful, no matter what their circumstances."

I glance over at my mom and dad, who are looking at me as if I am possessed. And I am. I am possessed with all the possibilities my future holds. Then I turn to the counselor. "Well, that's about all of the information I have about my life at this point in time. I still have work to do on myself, but one thing is certain: this particular event from my past will no longer haunt me. You have to admit, Sparky, so far my life is not bad for a guy who doesn't seem to have what it takes!"

Imagining this different scenario has empowered me to leave that nightmare experience behind. It is a relief to laugh at a part of my personal history that caused me so much pain and gives me the satisfaction of an "Ah-ha" moment.

Here's another example: the jackass on the interstate. When he cut you off 10 miles ago, you knew it was intentional and it pissed you off. Of course, 10 miles ago is 10 miles in the past. When you realize that something inconsequential is still upsetting you, rather than holding on to the negative emotions associated with the incident, think of the consequences of bringing those emotions to work or home with you. Doesn't sound very productive, does it? And it sure doesn't make any sense either.

Here's where the power of choice comes into play. You can simply shrug it off by shifting your perspective and focusing on more important issues like, "Boy, I'm happy I can drive without being a jackass," or "I have too many responsibilities today that need my full attention. I have to be at my emotional best. Why should I let one jackass ruin my entire day?" You feel a little better already, don't you? See what a little common sense and humor can do for you?

It really makes no difference whether something happened 20 minutes ago or 20 years ago. The past can be an absolutely irrelevant factor in our capacity to be at peace and to enjoy our lives now. Yet so many people hold on to their past struggles and use them as reasons for not being happy and successful. They create crippling beliefs that dictate what level of happiness the future holds for them. They become seduced by the voice inside their head and use their past struggles as a crutch and an excuse. It's impossible to be happy or at peace if your toxic past is following you everywhere you go and telling you who to be, what to do, and how to do it. Does it make sense to believe that you can never be happy, successful, or at peace *now* because of something that happened hours, days, or years ago? Of course not.

Maybe as a child you were abused by a parent or some other adult. Perhaps your parents divorced when you were young and you never received the love you deserved. Maybe you were made to feel that you didn't fit in or that you weren't smart enough to fulfill your dreams. Many children are raised in environments where anger and fear are the "normal" responses to challenging situations and everyday occurrences. Whatever your past experiences, I urge you to stop using your toxic past as an ID card to validate your right to proclaim your woe-is-me story to the world. Choose to break free now.

Our toxic past experiences no matter how severe are inconsequential in the present. It defies logic and common sense to hold on to emotional baggage like fear, anger, or guilt from hours, days, or years gone by. In fact, our past struggles can be our greatest blessings, if we learn from them and move on with our lives. Learning from our toxic past commends, while harboring it condemns. Stick that one on your refrigerator!

It all comes down to this: Do you want to live free in a higher state of consciousness in the present? Do you want beliefs that will empower you? Or do you want to be controlled by the unconscious ranting of the Big Mouth in your head? Negative thoughts and emotions are like unwanted visitors that refuse to leave. Every time you become aware of them and refuse to allow them in or throw them out before they can do any damage, you instill faith in yourself. You are victorious in keeping the Big Mouth at bay. Most important, step-by-step, a new you gradually begins to emerge. The trick is being aware on a continual basis. When you are in a state of awareness, higher thoughts prosper in your inner world, while toxic thoughts slowly dissipate.

When your desire to shift to the higher thoughts and feelings of joy, peace, and fulfillment become paramount in your life, awareness will come to you more quickly and more often. And so will your ability to shift to commonsense and humorous responses. The result: your identification with the Big Mouth inside your head will cease and the negative beliefs you have about yourself and the world around you will gradually change. In the end, the Big Mouth's voice is simply feedback, an amalgam of negative odds and ends that collect in everyone's mental drains over time. Then again, it could really be the devil.

ATTITUDE ADJUSTMENT STRATEGIES:

Practice shifting into a state of awareness.

The first step to freeing yourself from the Big Mouth inside your head is to be aware of it. As soon as you notice that you are unhappy or not feeling right and recognize it for what it is—the deceptive voice inside your head—you will begin to liberate yourself from identifying with the negativity it represents.

Practice using common sense and humor.

This habit is the second step to freeing yourself from the Big Mouth's wrath. As soon as you become aware of what the voice in your head is up to, say, "I know who you are and I know what you're trying to do." Then, depending on the situation, ask yourself commonsense questions or ask your Humor Being for guidance and rewrite your negative past experience into a comedy with a happy ending.

Laughter and the Fear Factor

> We have to be able to figure
> out how to laugh and cry at the
> same time.
>
> **FORMER NEW YORK CITY**
> **MAYOR RUDY GIULIANI**
> **at a post-9/11 press conference,**
> **announcing that he would still**
> **host *Saturday Night Live***

On the morning of September 11, 2001, I was on a flight from JFK Airport to Salt Lake City. I was going to give a speech to a group of 2,000 people on how to confront negative emotions by using their sense of humor as a tool. Little did I know that the morning of my scheduled talk, fear would be the dominating emotion to overtake our entire nation.

Although it took me years to write about this tragic, historical event, the memories still (and probably always will) stay with me as if it happened yesterday. My entire experience of 9/11, and the events that followed, confirmed what I already knew about fear and how to keep it from controlling our lives.

I remember I was talking to the woman next to me when our plane suddenly took a nosedive at a very fast speed. The captain announced there was an ATC (air traffic control) alert and we would be making an emergency landing in Omaha, Nebraska. When we landed, no one knew what was going on, and like millions of people around the world, we thought that a small plane had accidentally flown into the World Trade Center.

I walked over to the nearest lounge area and joined a group of people transfixed by what was happening on the television screen. The United States of America was under attack. Like many others around me, I found it impossible to process this horrifying truth. I knew what I was watching. I understood what I was hearing. But nonetheless it seemed unbelievable, like a scene from some big special effects movie. We watched the planes crashing into the towers and watched the towers falling. We saw the clips over and over, and at a certain point I wanted to yell out, "Okay, change the channel! I want to watch something else! This is scaring me!"

Of course it was. That was the purpose of the attack: to instill fear. And it worked. A somber silence filled the airport as people tried to reach their loved ones on cell phones and pay phones. All the lines were busy. Then came the announcement that the Omaha airport, as well as every other airport in the country, was closed indefinitely. This only added more pressure to an already intense situation.

I managed to get a room at a Days Inn, which was to be my place of residence for the next four days. Finally I was able to get through to my wife, Gina. I assured her that I was fine but that I would be stranded in Omaha for a few days. When she asked me if I really was okay, I said, "Well, I'm stranded in Omaha. I mean, why couldn't I be stranded in Hawaii or Florida? No, me, of course I'm stuck with the Children of the Corn!" We laughed and told each other, "I love you."

When I hung up the phone I realized how close I was to the situation. Let's face it, my plane left JFK Airport en route to Salt Lake

City about the same time as the ones the terrorists had taken over. I couldn't help but wonder if my plane had been considered as a potential weapon of destruction or whether there were terrorists on my flight who didn't have a chance to carry out their insane mission. And I was caught between two conflicting emotions. First, I was grateful for my life and thankful that my plane wasn't the terrorists' target. Second, I was mourning the loss of those who had died and for the loved ones who would be haunted by the memories of that day for the rest of their lives.

I began to contemplate whether I would ever be able to get on a plane again, and if so, how it would feel. That's right, I'm not ashamed to admit that I was experiencing what many others felt: abject fear. It had hit home. Fear of the unknown and fear of leaving my comfort zone. When I heard about terrorist attacks in other countries I remember thinking, "How awful," "What a terrible tragedy," or "Oh, those poor people!" But when the attack hit home, hard-core fear set in. The experience was no longer terrible, it was horrific. I knew without a doubt that the 9/11 tragedy had forever changed our reality, and our future survival would depend upon how we would deal with the fear factor.

Fear is always the number one force to confront when a catastrophic event or change takes place in our lives. Whether it's a faltering economy, the loss of a job, divorce, illness, or the death of a loved one, how we handle the fear factor will influence our quality of life. Know this: fear has eyes, ears, and a voice. We must be vigilant about what we say to ourselves when something unexpected or tragic happens. If we are constantly focusing on what's wrong with the situation and habitually thinking or blurting out loud, "Oh my God, this is horrible," we are creating an opening for fear's icy grip to take hold. In so doing, we feed fear the energy it needs to wreak even more havoc. "That neat little bubble you were in your whole life has blown up. And now there's hell to pay!" Unless you get your shift together and create a way to shift your perception about the situation at hand, fear, dread, and uncertainty will become a common sensation.

My second day in Omaha, I received a phone call from Power Talk Radio. The host, John St. Augustine, invited me to be a telephone guest along with renowned author and spiritual adviser Dr. Wayne Dyer, who at the time was also stranded ... in San Diego. My first thought was, "Oh, great. That figures. I'm hanging out in the farthest place from any beach in America and he gets San Diego."

They wanted Dr. Dyer and me to share our views on how to deal with the fear and chaos our country was experiencing. Dr. Dyer reminded us that there is a spiritual solution to every problem. I stressed the importance of making conscious choices to enjoy ourselves during the rebuilding process and finding the laughter in between and during the tough times. One of the points that I found most poignant was Dr. Dyer's response to those who were relating to the experience of 9/11 as being abnormal. Dr. Dyer simply said, "It is normal. It's just a new normal." After some reflection, I agreed. What transpired on 9/11 is normal. What is being done in the way of new security measures is normal. It's just a new normal. Life is always filled with the unexpected; it always has been. History shows that throughout time, events have taken place that dramatically impact the way people live: war, disease, famine, man-made and natural catastrophes, disasters, murder, and violence of all kinds have plagued the human race since the beginning of the world. These events happen in the "normal" course of human events. Whatever the future may hold, it will also come to be the "new" normal, because that's life and anything can happen.

One thing is certain: the protective bubble this country was living in has burst. More now than ever, biological, chemical, and nuclear warfare is a threat to world security. We are at the mercy of a group of religious fanatics who have no regard for human life, including their own, and whose mission in life is to instill fear. On top of all of this, we are in harsh economic times, political change, and a news media that constantly reminds us how bad and dangerous things are. Yes, we are all being forced to live a new normal. The ones who will ultimately prevail are those who will deal with the fear factor and adapt. I guarantee you, those who do adapt are the ones who make conscious choices to shift their focus, their beliefs, and their way of thinking. Guess what? Humor can help us to make the shifts that are necessary to move forward with hope and confidence.

"Laughter not only lifts the spirit; it is a natural pressure valve," says Larry Wilde, motivational speaker and author of over 50 books on humor. "When we're down in the dumps we need a boost, something to help us over the tough times. Smiles, chuckles, and old guffaws are a miraculous physical phenomenon that makes us feel good all over with the power to bring a twinkle to the eye and calm in the raging storm."

A few weeks after 9/11, I experienced an inward glow when I witnessed America's collective Humor Being helping us to shift our focus away from the pain. Osama bin Laden was being bombarded not only by airstrikes, but also by punch lines. Late-night television hosts like Jay Leno led the attack and helped us all to laugh off the fear.

Osama goes to a fortune-teller to find out how long he has to live. The fortune-teller informs him that he will die on a famous American holiday. "Which one?" bin Laden asks. "Whatever day you die will be a famous American holiday," the fortune-teller replies. The healing of America began to flourish the day we adjusted our attitudes and made the shift to laugh off the fear.

I believe we need our Humor Beings now more than at any time in the history of our planet. We need to allow ourselves to laugh when times are tough. It is crucial for us all to make conscious choices to enjoy ourselves during the transition to this new normal. If we allow fear in any situation to determine the choices we make, terror always wins, no matter what form it takes, whether it's an internal fear or an uncontrollable outside force. Today we need a strong foundation to stand on. Your Humor Being can help build that foundation.

Laughter is surely one of our greatest gifts. What good is a gift that we don't use? (The fruitcakes at Christmas don't count. Those are always best left uneaten.) I understand that there are times when your problems and concerns are so overwhelming that it feels disrespectful to laugh, you just don't want to laugh, or, for whatever reason, you just can't find it in you. I respect that. We've all been there. However, understand this: if at any time you're feeling you can't find the laughter, that's exactly when you need it the most. Just as mourning and grieving are essential in order to heal, so too is our ability to step away from the pain, even if only for a few moments, to seek the joy in other aspects of our lives. Sometimes, however, we get so caught up in an unfortunate circumstance that we don't realize that in the long run our very survival is dependent upon experiencing joy and laughter during and between life's tough times.

Some people don't allow themselves to laugh and enjoy their lives when times are tough because they feel guilty or feel they don't have the right. They say, "How can I find the laughter in my life when I was just diagnosed with cancer?" Well, that's when you're supposed to. They say, "How can you expect me to laugh and enjoy my life when the economy is falling apart and I may lose my job at any time?" Well, my friend, that's when you're supposed to. It is essential that we all understand that there is a difference between laughing at something that is serious and laughing off the fear it represents. I believe that's the number one reason why we are given the gift of laughter: to laugh in the face of fear. When you do, perception changes, negativity shifts, and fear is kept at bay. I want to make this point as clearly as I possibly can. Are you ready? When times are tough, even severe, we must at some point find the courage within ourselves to laugh off the fear.

If you've ever seen the hit television series *M*A*S*H*, you've witnessed numerous examples in each episode of what it means to laugh off the fear. The character Hawkeye, played by Alan Alda, has his Humor Being working overtime. Many times we observe him in the operating room exhausted without proper medical supplies. Sometimes bombs are exploding all around. The power is going on and off as his hands are in some soldier's body cavity, and blood is spurting all over the place. In the midst of all of this chaos, what do we find him doing? That's right. He's cracking jokes. But in cracking those jokes he's not negating the seriousness of the moment, not at all. Hawkeye intuitively knows that his sense of humor is the only saving grace in a place where there seems to be so little hope. In fact, his humor is giving him the strength, courage, and emotional fortitude to get the job done and save lives.

Now, some of you may think, "Great example, Steve, but get a grip. It's a television show. It's not real." That may be so, it is a television show, but the show and the movie *M*A*S*H* were actually based on the memoir of a real doctor who served in a MASH unit during the Korean War. Twisted humor of all kinds is used as an emotional shield to protect the military and civilians alike in times of war, just as a helmet or a shelter is used to keep their physical selves out of harm's way. My view is that this particular memoir was developed into "mass entertainment" because it depicts the type of humor often necessary to endure the perils of war and other tragedies.

Years ago I was watching Dan Rather interview Bill Cosby. It was a few weeks after his son's murder. After sharing his grief over his son's death, the comedian was asked, "Now that Bill Cosby's son is no longer with us, what is Bill Cosby going to do with the rest of his life?" Cosby contemplated the question for a few seconds and confidently said, "I think it's time for me to tell the people that we have to laugh. We've got to laugh. You can turn painful situations around through laughter. If you can find humor in anything, you can survive it." Read that again, my friend.

Hope Was Her Companion, Humor Was Her Shield

One morning some time ago, I was on a flight from New York to Nashville. Standing in the row adjacent to mine was an attractive woman wearing sunglasses. She was talking to two distinguished-looking men who (as I overheard from their conversation) were from MCA Records. I didn't know exactly what they were talking about, but obviously it was funny, because the laughter was nonstop. Even though I had no idea what was being said, I soon found myself joining in with their contagious laughter. When we were ready for takeoff, the woman with the sunglasses sat down next to me. She put her boarding pass on the armrest and I glanced at the name. As I had suspected, it was Naomi Judd. I looked over and told her how much I enjoyed her music. It wasn't a line. I may be from New York, but I love country music. Don't look so shocked. People come in all shapes and styles. Deal with it.

She smiled and said, "Thank you," and we began a wonderful conversation. She told me she had put her music career aside to speak to groups throughout the country on health and spirituality. I told her about being a comedian for 18 years and that I had segued into a speaking career focused on how to succeed in life and enjoy the process. I knew I had hit a sensitive spot, because she straightened up in her seat and said, "What a wonderful subject! How do you get people to enjoy their lives?" I looked right at her and said, "I tell them to take drugs." She let out one of her contagious laughs.

Our conversation continued, with both of us talking about our favorite comedians and sharing funny stories about being on the road. Eventually she told me about her life-threatening experience with hepatitis C. Apparently she was infected by pricking her finger with a needle years ago when she was working as a nurse. She was diagnosed in 1990, but a liver biopsy showed that she had contracted the disease six years earlier. Doctors didn't give her very long to live.

Since humor is obviously a core issue in my talks to groups, I asked her if her wonderful sense of humor helped her to release the fear caused by her ordeal. She laughed, reached down and grabbed hold of a big leather bag, and pulled out a whoopee cushion and other humorous paraphernalia. "Steve," she said with excitement, "I'm known as the goofiest woman in country music, and I'm proud of it!" At that moment, I saw the child within the woman, and I remember thinking, "This is indeed an individual who enjoys life to the fullest."

Our conversation took a more serious turn. Naomi told me that there were times when she felt that the life she had once loved was dwindling away. Being sick was not her style. She hated being in public in such a weak condition and felt the need to be around people who could make her laugh. But still she kept reaching for some kind of hope, which she described as an open window with a light shining through. And she instinctively relied on her sense of humor to help her get through the tough times.

When she arrived at the world-famous Mayo Clinic she was weak and scared. They put her into a wheelchair and told her she was going to the admitting office. Her reply was, "You can take me where you want, but I ain't admittin' to nothin'!"

At one point, she met with a new doctor for a second opinion. "Your enzymes are higher than ever," he said, with all the warmth of a glacier. "The active inflammation going on in your liver is destroying the hepatic cells. Now, these dead cells will turn into scar tissue called cirrhosis. The damage is irreversible. Cirrhosis usually turns into cancer, but before that, various parts of the liver will begin shutting down. So it's hard to say which one will actually be your demise."

Her response was, "How about them Dodgers?" When the doctor said he needed to see her back in a week, she said, "Nope. You shoved me out of an airplane at 35,000 feet without giving me anything to break my fall. I'm going to find a doctor who will give me a parachute. It's called hope."

It was this type of attitude and quick wit that kept Naomi Judd from falling apart. It helped her control the fear that threatened to consume her. She told me that her sense of humor somehow always managed to help her reconnect to her spiritual side. It was that connection that gave her hope to move forward in spite of fear. Hope was her constant companion. Humor was her shield. Together this dynamic duo helped her to derail fear and embrace the power of love.

Here is a personal story about how using humor as your shield can derail fear and help you embrace the power of love. Years ago my mom had to undergo major surgery. A week before the surgery, the family met with a specialist to review hospital procedures and to answer any questions we had regarding the operation.

When the doctor walked into his office, he stopped in midstride when he saw the crowd that was waiting for him. Apparently he was only expecting my mom and dad, not the entire Rizzo family: my wife and me, my two brothers and their wives, my sister and her husband, and of course, Mom and Dad. Believe me, the Brady Bunch we're not! I have a brother named Rocky. Rocky Rizzo. Need I say more?

I suppose having all of us in one small room only added tension to an already stressful situation. From the doctor's perspective it probably felt more like an interrogation than a consultation. After we introduced ourselves the doctor proceeded to ask my mom some questions. "Do you have any problems hearing?" he asked.

Mom had a wonderful sense of humor and decided this was a good time to take advantage of it. "What?" she replied.

We all tried to hold back the laughter. But the doctor didn't get it. He repeated the question, only louder. "DO YOU HAVE ANY PROBLEMS HEARING?"

"NO! AND WHY ARE YOU YELLING?" she replied. At that point we all broke out laughing.

The doctor sat back in his chair, shook his head, laughed, and said, "Oh, it's gonna be one of those days."

"Stop whining!" Mom said. "I'm the one who needs the surgery!"

I remember thinking, "Oh my God, she's on a roll!"

The doctor continued asking questions. "Do you have a problem with memory loss?"

Mom thought about it and said, "No." Then she leaned toward the doctor and whispered, "But can you tell me who all these people are and why I'm here?"

Mom's ability to make us laugh put all of us at ease, including the doctor. As a result we were able to break down that wall of fear and ask important questions regarding the surgery.

As I look back on my life I can honestly say that it was always the spirit of love that pulled us through, but it was the power of laughter that kept us from falling apart.

In her book *Love Can Build a Bridge*, Naomi writes, "Love is the greatest healing power of all. There is nothing that comes close." She also says, "Hope is a gift we give to ourselves. It remains when all else is gone. It guides us beyond doubt and keeps us from sinking in our fears. It helps us picture the way we want things to be, so we can bring them about."

I agree. Love is the greatest healing power of all. Hope is a gift we give to ourselves. Our sense of humor is also a gift. It, too, fills us with unlimited healing powers. As with love and hope, humor is something we must choose to let into our lives. If we choose to make the shift and view our problems, challenges, and even our tragedies from a humorous perspective, we can prevent fear and other negative emotions from taking over.

If hope was Naomi Judd's parachute, then humor was the force that helped her take that leap of faith, and love was the foundation she landed on. With these dynamics at work, anyone can overcome insurmountable odds.

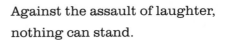

Way Beyond Comedy

> Against the assault of laughter,
> nothing can stand.
>
> **MARK TWAIN**

When I give my talks, people often ask, "What is it about comedians that separate them from everyone else?" My answer is simple: it's the way we look at life. A comedian views life and all of its obstacles, tragedies, mistakes, and embarrassing moments from an absurd or humorous perspective. I go on to explain that in doing so, we are not negating the seriousness of the subject matter, but rather looking at it from a different perspective, the humor perspective.

Let me share with you one of the key factors that motivated me to leave stand-up comedy and move on to the speaking forum. Following a comedy performance, I would often feel a huge surge of positive energy that made me feel like I could accomplish anything. Sometimes after the show, I would go back to my hotel room to write in my journal or put together material for a new routine. I literally felt this surge power through my whole body and my creative juices flow through me, into the pen and onto the paper. Other times I would go out with a group of people, party, laugh, and have fun. The point is that whatever I did after the show, all negative thoughts were banished, and whatever problems I had at the time seemed manageable. I was in the moment and enjoying it to the fullest.

Initially I thought these power surges were a function of my ego, stimulated by the rush of standing ovations, signing autographs, and people wanting to be around me. Although all of these things definitely made me feel good, I knew there was something more to it. Then one night at a show it hit me. My life was at an all-time low. I was either in a full-blown depression or on the brink of one. All of the old fears and limiting beliefs that I thought I had conquered had come back to haunt me.

That night, it took everything I had to muster up enough energy and courage to step onto the stage. I remember thinking how ironic life is. I mean, there I was, waiting to perform before a sold-out crowd of over five hundred people who wanted nothing more than to laugh and have a good time, when all I wanted to do was cry. That night I got real honest and spent two hours on that stage ranting about how my life sucked. Much to my surprise, the crowd loved it and couldn't get enough. In spite of how I felt—or maybe because of how I felt—I had one of the most spectacular performances of my career.

When I finally stepped off the stage the euphoria hit me with more intensity than ever before. I remember saying to myself, "This is way beyond comedy." I felt the invincible power of confidence and hope. It was then that I understood what this power surge of positive energy was all about. When I was up onstage, I shifted into a totally different state of mind. Don't get freaked out here, but there were times when I actually felt myself shift to a higher realm of consciousness, a place where the Big Mouth had no power. And of course, when shift happens, your life changes.

That night I did more than my usual act. I let my Humor Being loose and allowed my higher self to take control. I talked about some painful experiences from my past. I literally laughed off my frustrations, pain, negative labels, and innermost fears. I vented my anger in a constructive way and the crowd loved it. It was like therapy, with two major differences: it was fun to do, and I didn't have to pay for it.

A few days later, I began to reflect on what happened onstage that night. Without my knowledge, the owner of the club had recorded my entire performance. It felt strange listening to the recording and hearing myself rant and rave about my personal problems and history in such an intimate way. Although I'm not one to avoid speaking my mind, I knew that what went on that night was beyond that. If I didn't know better, I would have thought that someone had slipped me some kind of truth serum that made me reveal parts of myself that I had never showed before.

I now know that it was my Humor Being pushing me forward (a part of my higher self that worked to expose my fears for what they were: nothing more than toxic data from my past). Through humor I was able to shift into a higher state of consciousness. At that moment I experienced a profound, secure feeling that my negative labels and the fears that belonged to them would no longer influence me or define my reality.

I also came to understand that the reason the audience enjoyed themselves so much was because they were laughing at a part of themselves. In other words, my stories, and the humor behind them, helped the members of the audience to view their own personal problems from a healthier perspective. I guess you could say our Humor Beings were communing. We were feeding off of each other, all five hundred and one of us. That's another thing humor does—it makes us realize that in the universal scheme of things, we are all made of the same stuff. We all have fears, pain, heartaches, and personal problems to deal with. We just have different stories to tell. It doesn't matter who you are, what you do, or how much money you make. It doesn't matter if you're black or white, male or female, rich or poor, conservative or liberal, gay or straight. We all make mistakes. We all have our successes and failures. And we all have good times and bad. Humor simply helps us embrace who we really are and gives us the peace to live with it.

One could certainly argue that if humor is so healing, then why didn't it help Lenny Bruce, John Belushi, Chris Farley, Richard Pryor, and many other comedy greats? I suggest that these extremely talented funny men were hiding behind the humor. They used the comedy arena as an escape from their problems and as a mask to cover them up. This distinction is worth mentioning, since it is a common practice among people in all walks of life. Using humor as a means to coax problems into a different light in which to examine them is positive. Hiding behind laughter can most certainly have negative, and even dangerous, consequences because of the false impression it can give to others and oneself that everything is okay, when in reality there may be a lifetime of unresolved pain, fear, and anger behind it.

If you are unable to face and come to terms with that which is destroying your inner core, you can end up living a lie—and laughter is an easy way to cover up that lie. Ironically, those who feed the lie with laughter are usually the ones whom everybody loves. They're the life of the party. They're always cracking jokes, and they will go out of their way to make people laugh. We all know people like this. They're the "good-time Charlies" who don't seem to have a care in the world. But quite often the so-called good-time Charlie consumes a great deal of alcohol and drugs, which helps him to hide behind the laughter all the more. One could say that laughter in itself becomes a kind of drug to good-time Charlie, who partakes in it for the high that it offers. He depends on it to give him temporary relief and escape. Unfortunately, when used this way, laughter has no healing effect whatsoever. In fact, every time the truth tries to reveal itself, the Big Mouth inside your head jumps in and says, "It's okay!

You're okay! Forget that empty feeling. You're not afraid. You're not angry. You're not insecure! You're in total control! You have money. You're a great success. Everybody loves you! What else could you possibly need? Hey, I'll tell you what you need. You need to loosen up. You need more drugs, more alcohol! That's what you need. That's it, now crack a few more jokes. Go ahead, make 'em laugh! There now, you see? I told you! Don't you feel better?"

The comedy greats that I mentioned above had their own unique gift to give to the world. As funny as they were, however, I believe that none of them were able to use humor as a transformational tool in the healing process. In other words, they weren't using humor to confront their issues. They were using humor to hide from them. In order for any of us to solve our problems or heal from any ailment or addiction, we must first become aware of what needs fixing and admit that there is a problem. Once there is awareness, the healing process can begin. With awareness comes the opportunity to take action to better yourself. When used properly, humor can help you to confront your demons and deepest fears.

The moment you start laughing in the face of fear, you instantly shift into a higher state of awareness or consciousness and can tap into your own power. This shift to awareness stops the bombardment of negative thoughts and exposes the liar (the Big Mouth) within for what it really is: nothing more than fear-based negative beliefs from past experiences that you are bringing into the present. Yes, it's true that this shift to awareness may only last a few moments. But (and it's a big but—no, I'm not talking about your big *butt*. I mean the other big *but*, so give me a break!) those few moments can give you enough time, hope, and courage to view your problem or fear from a healthier perspective. Remember, whenever you laugh in the face of any problem or fear, you create a shift in your awareness. This shift, I believe, instantly overpowers the ranting of the Big Mouth and connects you to your higher self. Holy shift!

Emotional Self-Defense

One Saturday night years ago, I was performing at the Comedy
Store in Los Angeles. The place was sold out, standing room only. I
was backstage talking to a fellow comedian, also named Steve. We
were discussing what a trip it was to make people laugh and, better
yet, get paid for it. We agreed that the power of laughter has many
medicinal purposes. I suggested that since we were responsible for
making people laugh, perhaps we shouldn't be called comedians.
Maybe we should be known as "Humor Healing Technicians."

The conversation took on a more serious tone when Steve told
me that he was HIV positive. Now, you need to understand that
this was in 1992 and the HIV virus was a much bigger threat than
it is today. I asked how he was dealing with it. His response was,
"Watch me."

"What?" I asked.

"I'm going on before you," he said. "Watch my set."

I went to the back of the room and stood next to some of
the other comedians. Steve was introduced and launched into his
routine—"Hi, I'm Steve, and I'm HIV positive. Don't be concerned.
Naomi Judd was diagnosed with chronic hepatitis C. The good
news is that we're going to form a duo and call ourselves 'Sick and
Tired'!" He spent the next 20 minutes on the HIV virus, but from
that opening moment he had the entire audience in the palm of
his hand.

Steve's Humor Being was glowing that night. His comic tim-
ing was spot on, equaled only by the powerful message that was in-
terwoven in and around the laughter. He even found humor in the
many side effects that occurred from all the different medications
he was taking. There were over five hundred people in that room
and Steve had them laughing their butts off. More important, he
made them realize how healing laughter can be and how precious

life truly is. I remember saying to one of the comedians, "This guy is making people laugh about one of the biggest challenges to face this planet!"

Later that evening our conversation continued. I told Steve that I admired his courage and found his routine to be absolutely mind-blowing. He smiled and said, "Thank you, but do you want to hear the best news of all?"

"Yeah," I said.

"My white blood cell count has gone up phenomenally ever since I chose to deal with this challenge with humor."

I stood there with my mouth open, searching for the proper words. Finally, all I could think to say was, "That's incredible."

Later on in his career, Steve starred in his own HBO special entitled *HIV* and developed quite a following. His humor and the message behind it inspired people who were HIV positive to embrace their challenge rather than run from it.

I want to reiterate an important point. We all know that there is nothing funny about the HIV virus. Steve was not laughing at his challenge. Nor was he hiding behind the laughter or using it to cover up the lie. He very simply used his sense of humor as a tool to laugh off the fear of the challenge. This in turn created a shift in his awareness. This higher state of awareness enabled Steve to confront his challenge directly. When confronting his fear he gradually began to understand where it was coming from and why it was controlling his life. Understanding then led to compassion, and compassion led to the ultimate, unconditional love for himself and for life.

One of the greatest turning points in my life came when I realized that I didn't have to be the comedian onstage to deal with my fear, anger, or other negative emotions. I discovered that my Humor Being is just as powerful and effective offstage as it is on. Gradually, I made conscious efforts to shift my perspective to find the humor in whatever challenging and stressful situation I was in. Today, I view my problems as manageable. My bouts with anger don't last as long and my fears and the Big Mouth inside my head don't overwhelm me. When I pause, ask myself any number of reasonable questions, and take the time to laugh, I realize that the choices I make impact how I feel and render my problems manageable.

Telling yourself that you have a choice and knowing that your thoughts create your reality puts you in a position to view your challenges from a distance. As a bystander, it's a lot easier to see the potential consequences if you allow a negative state to take you over. And it is easier to interject humor into the situation. Even a little levity can help change your perception of a particular problem. Humor is your natural defense mechanism. It's a prescription from your Humor Being (a part of your higher self) to cure the emotional chaos that attacks you from day to day. To deny yourself the right to find the humor in the midst of all the chaos is like denying yourself treatment that can cure an illness. So, for crying out loud, do yourself a favor and laugh.

> ### ATTITUDE ADJUSTMENT STRATEGY:
> **Make a conscious effort to find the humor in all challenging situations.**
>
> The moment you start laughing in the face of even your greatest fear, you instantly shift into a higher state of awareness.

High Points to Remember

- Stop using your toxic past as an ID card to validate your right to proclaim your woe-is-me story to the world.

Practice awareness and choose to break free from the Big Mouth inside your head now.

- Suffering may be unavoidable, but adding to your pain by remaining in a prolonged negative state can be. Finding the laughter in between and during the tough times is essential to living a happier life.

- Fear is always the number one force to confront when a drastic event or change takes place in your life. Unless you find a way to shift your perception about the situation at hand, you will never truly win over it.

- It's essential to understand that there is a difference between laughing at something that is serious and laughing off the fear that it represents.

- The more you make the shift to use your sense of humor as a tool to confront your challenges, the more it will become a part of who you are, and the more emotionally balanced you will become.

Make the Commitment Now

No matter what your current circumstances, making happiness your number one priority is a necessary step that you can achieve. After all, you want to achieve happiness more than anything else, whether you feel you've earned it or not. When you become aware of this fact and incorporate the Attitude Adjustment Strategies outlined in this book, you will be truly amazed at the many positive effects you'll experience at work and in life. Committing to making happiness a habit is key. Follow through with determination to seize opportunities to do so, and you will see a huge difference in how your daily life unfolds.

We constantly find ourselves in serious situations that can drain the happiness from us and undermine the feeling that we deserve happiness now. Despite the burden these situations can have on our body, mind, and spirit, despite the intense moments of fear, self-doubt, guilt, anger, and many other negative emotions, it is all part of the human experience. The big question is to what extent will you allow these negative emotions to consume you? Will you let them dictate the choices you make and the actions you take? Will you allow them to regulate the degree of your overall happiness? Don't be a victim of your emotions. Get your shift together, employ a Power Shift in Focus, and give them a piece of your mind.

Although people operate on different clocks, it's imperative that you allow yourself to rebound from challenging situations and pay attention to the aspects of your life that lift you up and empower you. Life goes on, regardless of what happens to you or around you, so why not make the best of it? This is something successful, happy, and optimistic people know about life. The good news is that you have a choice. This, too, is part of being human.

When happiness becomes a habit, you will be able to weather the storms of chaos and misfortune with the knowledge that while your circumstances may not be ideal, your attitude is.

The longer you remain unhappy, the greater the opportunity for negative emotions to control your state of mind. If you make the grave mistake of allowing your circumstances to dictate the degree of your overall happiness, then you run the risk of missing out on the joy and success that life has to offer.

Remember, the more you concentrate on what you lack, the more of it you will get back. The more you focus on what is failing, the more your life won't work.

Remember, the more you focus on what is working in your life, the more you appreciate what you have, the more you elevate your degree of overall happiness.

That is the single most important lesson I've learned, and I learned it the hard way. In fact, I learned most things the hard way. (Especially when asked, "Does this make me look fat?" There is no right answer to this question, so don't fall into its trap. It's a trick! Don't ever answer that question! Just shake your head emphatically and back away slowly.) But the truth is, I have learned most of my life lessons the hard way. And *that* is why I'm writing this book. I hope reading it will make your life a little easier.

By now you should believe without a doubt that you can increase your degree of overall happiness, no matter what is currently happening in your life. You can make moment-to-moment choices to enjoy yourself during the process of whatever it is you are trying to achieve. Remember, your Humor Being is of your higher self. It's the part of you that brings out the best in you when times are tough. Acknowledge its power at all times. And, please, don't forget to laugh throughout the course of a day. Especially when it seems your world is falling apart, and powerful negative emotions are closing in on you, muster up the courage to shift your focus, thoughts, and beliefs. Connect to your natural state of joy and inner peace, the place where the God part of you, the divine, life force, higher self, or whatever you want to call it, resides. When you make happiness a habit, you will find yourself a frequent traveler to that place and your desires and dreams will manifest to their full potential with greater ease.

As Benjamin Franklin observed, the Declaration of Independence only gives people the *right* to pursue happiness. You have to catch it yourself.

About the Author

Steve Rizzo (www.steverizzo.com) is a personal development expert who addresses more than 50,000 people annually through his speaking engagements. As a professional keynote and motivational speaker, Steve has made appearances internationally. His clients include American Airlines, JPMorgan Chase, Scholastic, Sprint, and many others. He has appeared on MSNBC, CNBC, and the Oprah and Friends Radio Network, as well as his own PBS special, *Becoming a Humor Being*. He was also inducted into the Speaker Hall of Fame and was voted a Showtime Comedy All-Star. Prior to his speaking career, Steve was a headline stand-up comedian, sharing the stage with comic greats such as Jerry Seinfeld, Ellen DeGeneres, Eddie Murphy, and Rodney Dangerfield, among others. He lives in New York City.